Darkness Is My Only Companion

A CHRISTIAN RESPONSE TO MENTAL ILLNESS

Kathryn Greene-McCreight

BrazosPress

a division of Baker Publishing Group
Grand Rapids, Michigan

© 2015 by Kathryn Greene-McCreight

Published by Brazos Press
a division of Baker Publishing Group
P.O. Box 6287, Grand Rapids, MI 49516-6287
www.brazospress.com

Printed in the United States of America

Library of Congress Cataloging-in-Publication Data
Greene-McCreight, Kathryn, 1961–
    Darkness is my only companion : a Christian response to mental illness / Kathryn Green-McCreight.— Revised and expanded.
        pages cm
    Includes bibliographical references.
    ISBN 978-1-58743-372-6 (pbk.)
    1. Mental illness—Religious aspects—Christianity. 2. Mentally ill—Religious life. I. Title.
    RC455.4.R4G74 2015
    616.89—dc23   2015007843

15   16   17   18   19   20   21   7   6   5   4   3   2   1

Praise for the First Edition

"By means of personal story, theological reflection, and practical suggestions for caregivers, Greene-McCreight takes readers into her mind as she plunges from frantic ecstasy . . . to profound despair. . . . With firm but never facile faith, she offers hope to Christians with mental illness and understanding to those who live and work with them."

—Publishers Weekly (starred review)

"This book is a real gem. While brutally honest about the darkest experiences a human can suffer, it is nonetheless both hopeful and encouraging for anyone who either suffers from a serious mental illness or seeks to help someone who does. I heartily recommend it and expect it will have a long and fruitful life."

—David G. Benner, author of *Presence and Encounter*

"Kathryn Greene-McCreight gives to us a rare gift: a glimpse of God at work intimately in a human life, powerfully in the church, and mysteriously in the world. Her remarkable reflections are both theologically astute and self-consciously framed within the Great Tradition of the church."

—Edith M. Humphrey, author of *Ecstasy and Intimacy: When the Holy Spirit Meets the Human Spirit*

"Theologically sound and medically astute, this is a safe guide for those who battle the darkness of mental illness and for those who care about them. . . . [Greene-McCreight] does what is so desperately needed in our therapeutic society—she practices psychotherapy under the authority of Scripture. A careful theologian, fully committed to the authority of Scripture, yet the beneficiary of healing therapy with an astonishingly wide and deep understanding of the field, the author weds the two convincingly."

—**Robertson McQuilkin**, *Christianity Today*

"[A] sensitive and profound work. . . . All of [Greene-McCreight's] observations are grounded in Scripture and the Christian tradition, and offer hope and help to the increasing number of Christians who recognize that her story is theirs as well."

—**L. P. Fairfield**, *Touchstone*

My everlasting gratitude to
Matthew, whose love is beyond measure;
Noah and Grace, for their joy;
Bob and Joyce, my first theological teachers;
Alex, for her steady friendship;
Pam M., for her prayers;
Barbara, for her strength.
For those who were indeed companions in the darkness,
I will always be grateful.

*Ad majorem Dei gloriam
et aedificationem ecclesiae.*

Contents

Foreword to the Second Edition

I must begin with a confession. I only began to read Kathryn Greene-McCreight's book because my friend and colleague N. T. (Tom) Wright asked me to do so. Since one of my own children began to blog and tweet about her own experience of mental illness, the daily experience has been of strangers writing and suggesting that they have come up with the book, treatment, diet, or other solution that solves the problem right away. One begins to get a little cynical. And so when Tom wrote to me asking me to look at this book, I felt that he might have been succumbing to the same problem.

How wrong I was. Kathryn Greene-McCreight does not set out to provide solutions but writes one of the most profound and eye-opening reflections on the grace and love of God, and above all on the nature of human relationships, that I have had the pleasure of reading.

Where is God when all is dark, not through the mystical dark night of the soul of St. John of the Cross (memorably examined in chap. 10) but because something in one's own brain has become an enemy? God has not withdrawn, yet darkness has intruded and has become the only companion, as the psalmist writes in Psalm 88.

The nature of mental illness is to remove one from the normal constraints, perceptions, and understandings of the world around, whatever one's rational self may say. It is not merely a question of feeling but of the world being a different sort of place in all one's perceptions. The struggle this brings, and with the struggle the disassociation from those around one, is profound and utterly overwhelming. In the first part of the book, Kathryn recalls and reflects on her own experience of this struggle in a very extreme form. I have seen it in those I love and find myself pitched by the book into a place of greater understanding and sympathy than I had experienced before.

At its most extreme form, mental illness literally changes the perception of the world around. Roads become like mist; the feelings and desires of one's body become not merely overwhelming but determinant of one's behavior. How then do we understand sin? Where is the power of the Holy Spirit to deliver us and set us free? Then at the same time, our relationships change. Love may still come to us constantly but will not be felt and understood as love or as anything that is recognizable. Mental illness changes us.

The church has never been good at examining what this does to people's perception of who God is or what it means to be a faithful Christian. When we cannot understand, how can we obey? Kathryn roots her answers in the Psalms, and above all in the nature of truly gracious relationships. Such grace may be experienced in a hospital, through medical practitioners and therapists, through family who go on loving when the person one has loved seems to have taken leave of absence, and above all through God. In the midst of the howling gale of illness—when all the normal navigation points that enable one to understand where one is with people and with God have ceased to be reliable—even so, relationships remain. For me, that has been the greatest blessing of this book, a new understanding of what it means to say that Jesus is the same yesterday, today, and forever. It has also renewed in me hope in the reality of Christian healing. Kathryn discusses the nature of prayer for healing and recalls her own experience of a moment of being prayed for as—to some extent and without great drama—a turning point. I found my own faith renewed—deepened—and my own hopes expanded through the beauty of her writing.

So, this is in the end a book about relationship. Full relationships are those of love that does not change when the one loved is profoundly altered. In such relationships we see most deeply the nature of God. They draw us out of ourselves and perhaps begin in a strange way to give faint echoes of a response to the troubles and divisions of the church in a multicultural world. What does God do when we fail? God goes on loving. What does God do when the church collectively appears to be ill? God goes on loving. The reconciliation of God, I have learned afresh from this book, is overwhelmingly more powerful than all the brokenness of my humanity.

And so I am grateful to Tom for suggesting the read, to Kathryn for her beautiful book and for inviting me to write its foreword, and above all to the God who unexpectedly has renewed in me his perfect love and grace.

+Justin Cantuar
St. Patrick's Day 2014

Preface to the First Edition

This project examines the distress caused and the Christian theological questions raised by a clinical mental illness, namely, mine. This is therefore on the one hand a highly personal book, since it in part tells my own story. Yet on the other hand it is also theological and pastoral insofar as it deals with questions raised by the Christian theological tradition. These questions center on the topics of sin and grace, creation and redemption, God's discipline of the soul, the hiddenness of God, and the dark night of the soul. It is my hope that the book also will provide practical advice for clergy and friends in dealing with mentally ill parishioners, friends, and family.

This book has grown for many years. I began writing in the midst of a manic episode in 1998 and returned to composition later, again and again. I have not recounted every episode of every illness, only those episodes that might be helpful to the reader. After all, this book is finally not *about* my own mental illness but my theological reflections on mental illness.

I include throughout the book bits of Scripture and quotations from great figures of the Christian tradition to show how the great cloud of witnesses (Heb. 12:1) helped, supported, and encouraged me in my illnesses. These are integral to the book, not just frosting. As I state in appendix I, "Why and How I Use Scripture," I drank from Scripture throughout my illness in a way that was finally traditional in scope and practice, and healing in promise. The translation of Scripture used is the New Revised Standard Version (NRSV), and the translation of the Psalms is from the Book of Common Prayer (1979), except where indicated.

A note on language: I do not, as a policy, adopt "inclusive language" in reference to God. This term disrupts its own definition when we use it for the Godhead. The claim of feminist theologians here is that, as Mary Daly says, "if God is male, then male is God."[1] If Daly's statement is true, then, so the claim goes, referring to God in masculine terms gives patriarchy divine sanction. Therefore, according to Daly's logic, we must not use masculine terms or pronouns to refer to God. Many feminists would not use the terms *Father* and *Son*, for example, to speak of the first and second persons of the Trinity.[2] Women, it is said, must be included in the Godhead just as men are.

However, it is not the nature of the Christian God to "include" either males or females within its being in this way. I use inclusive language only for humanity, since there is nothing in the reality of God that allows us, whether male or female, the luxury of being "included" in the first place. Since God is generally referred to in the Bible with the pronoun *he*, this is also the pronoun I generally use to refer to God. I thereby suggest neither that God is male nor that the female is "underrepresented" and the male "overrepresented" in the Godhead.

When you see the word LORD in my text, this points to the Tetragrammaton as in the biblical text, the four-letter unpronounceable name of the God of Exodus 3:15. This will be important in particular in the quotations from the Psalms. Here the name means "he is who he is," or "he will be what he will be," or "he brings into being what he brings into being." It is sometimes transliterated by the word *Yahweh* or *Jehovah* in different translations. *Lord* (capitalized *L* and lowercase *ord*) in the New Testament usually refers to Jesus, along with the pronoun *he*. Clearly Jesus was a man. *Lord* can also mean something more like "sir" but also can refer to God.

I try to use the feminine pronouns *she/her* to refer to the generic patient, the priest, and sometimes the therapist. I use the masculine pronoun to refer to the generic doctor but only to avoid confusing the doctor with the patient. I am not suggesting thereby that only women have mental illnesses or that only men are doctors. This is simply a way to use inclusive language for people in a way that is meaningful for this particular book.

The reader should note that this book is not intended to be a medical manual, taking the place of medical advice. Although it does contain medical information, nothing should take the place of seeing your doctor if you find yourself exhibiting any of the symptoms mentioned. For the full diagnostic criteria of major depression and bipolar disorder, see Kay Redfield Jamison's fine book *Touched with Fire*.[3] See also appendix II below for diagnostic criteria for major depression, bipolar disorder, and schizophrenia.

To those who read drafts of this book and gave me comments, I am grateful: Nancy Brennan, Laird and Sally Edman, Greg Ganssle, Joyce and Robert Greene, Marvin Greene, Steve Horst, Matthew McCreight, Ephraim Radner and Annette Brownlee, Jana and Ron Rittgers, and Michael and Carol Tessman. Many thanks to Rodney Clapp for his encouragement, sensitivity, and critical eye. Thanks also to Paul Stuehrenberg from Yale Divinity Library for the Research Affiliates Program, which allowed me the facilities to research this project.

O LORD, my God, my Savior,
    by day and night I cry to you.
Let my prayer enter into your presence;
    incline your ear to my lamentation.
For I am full of trouble;
    my life is at the brink of the grave.
I am counted among those who go down to the Pit;
    I have become like one who has no strength;
Lost among the dead,
    like the slain who lie in the grave,
Whom you remember no more,
    for they are cut off from your hand.
You have laid me in the depths of the Pit,
    in dark places, and in the abyss.
Your anger weighs upon me heavily,
    and all your great waves overwhelm me.
You have put my friends far from me;
    you have made me to be abhorred by them;
    I am in prison and cannot get free.
My sight has failed me because of trouble;
    LORD, I have called upon you daily;
    I have stretched out my hands to you.

Do you work wonders for the dead?
    will those who have died stand up and give you thanks?
Will your loving-kindness be declared in the grave?
    your faithfulness in the land of destruction?
Will your wonders be known in the dark?
    or your righteousness in the country where all is
        forgotten?
But as for me, O LORD, I cry to you for help;
    in the morning my prayer comes before you.
LORD, why have you rejected me?
    why have you hidden your face from me?
Ever since my youth, I have been wretched and at the point
        of death;
    I have borne your terrors with a troubled mind.
Your blazing anger has swept over me;
    your terrors have destroyed me;
They surround me all day long like a flood;
    they encompass me on every side.
My friend and my neighbor you have put away from me,
    and darkness is my only companion.

Psalm 88

Introduction

No testing has overtaken you that is not common to
everyone. God is faithful, and he will not let you be
tested beyond your strength, but with the testing he
will also provide the way out so that you may be able
to endure it.

1 Corinthians 10:13

I have struggled with clinical mental illness for the last quarter
of my life. In fact, I seem to have had my first depression, then
undiagnosed, as a child of twelve years. Minor lows and highs followed throughout my adolescence, but the first diagnosed major
clinical depression was a postpartum episode after my second
child was born, thirteen years ago now, when I was in graduate
school. That depression lasted a few years, on and off. About five
years later I had a manic episode, which changed the diagnosis to
bipolar disorder. This is a disease that bounces between depression and mania. Major depression again followed on the heels of
the manic episode, and over the next few years I was hospitalized
five times and given two courses of electroconvulsive therapy for
major depression. Some five years after I was diagnosed bipolar,

my doctor and I finally stumbled upon the right "cocktail" for my brain, and I have steadily improved, avoiding depression and mania since then.

During this time, I have read much of the literature geared to the layperson on mental illness, eagerly searching for a book that would answer, or at least address, my questions: Does God send this suffering? If so, why? And why this particular kind of suffering? Why, if I am a Christian, can I not rejoice? What is happening to my soul?

I found no books among the latest offerings that addressed such questions, and books by Christian authors were often dismissive of the soul's agony in mental illness, and of psychotherapy in general. Most of the books answered scientific questions, which were in themselves not uninteresting to me. However, I wanted a book that would ask not purely scientific questions about these illnesses and symptoms but religious questions, and not just any religious questions but specifically Christian theological questions. What are the realities of suffering and evil when viewed from the Christian gospel? How might a Christian respond in the face of mental illness? How is the soul affected by the disease of the mind, indeed a disease of the brain? Does the Christian tradition offer resources for coping with mental illness and for explaining its origin and its healing?

I do not intend to search out and ground philosophical consistency for "solving" the problem of evil. I am no philosopher, and even philosophers can't "solve" problems, much less the problem of evil. I am concerned instead to offer a biblically grounded account, from my own experience, of how the Christian may interpret, accept, and handle suffering, especially that with such a stigma as mental illness. The Christian who lives with a mental illness will not be helped much by a philosophical discussion of free will, for example. My concern instead is to offer theological resources for interpreting and surviving mental illness. When I found no book to address my questions, I realized that I myself would have to write it.

This book began, then, as my own agonizing search for the meaning of my mental illness. I hesitated to make this autobiographical; the genre of psychobiography is well represented on the shelves of any bookstore. Instead, I wanted to struggle with the theological meanings, if I could even find any, of a mental illness such as my own. How could I, as a faithful Christian, be undergoing such torture of the soul? And how could I say that such torture has nothing to do with God? This is, of course, the assumption within the psychiatric guild in general, where faith in "God" is often viewed at best as a crutch and at worst as a symptom of disease.[1]

This is only beginning to change, with many studies indicating that religious practice or "spiritual" life can actually help healing of mental illnesses. These studies, however, also indicate that religious people "are less stressed and happier than non-believers" and that "religious people are less depressed, less anxious and less suicidal than nonreligious people."[2] This only plays into the caricature of the Christian as perennially cheery. It is a cruel caricature for those Christians who are indeed depressed or experiencing other symptoms of mental illnesses. Often they feel guilty on top of being depressed, because they understand their depression, their lack of thankfulness, their desperation, to be a betrayal of God. And yet these studies say nothing of the objectivity of God's involvement in mental illness. How could they, being written by scientists and not theologians? They simply deal with the objectivity of *belief* in God. For Christians, mentally ill or healthy, if our *belief* in God takes precedence over God himself in our theology and our devotion, we run the risk of worshiping ourselves. This is one of the pitfalls of modern theology and the principle cancer of much of Protestant Christianity in the West. Furthermore, if we focus on our own belief rather than on God, and if we find that we have no belief, which is often how Christians living with mental illnesses experience ourselves, we are in danger of getting sucked into and trapped by our own interiority. We end up with the potential for self-isolation but also for self-worship, which is pastorally and theologically a pitfall to be avoided at all costs. And especially for the Christian facing mental illness, this is exceedingly dangerous. If we are the center of our universe and of our worship, we are, in the words of the apostle, "most to be pitied" (1 Cor. 15:19). For this reason and others, I find these studies and their apparent outcomes to do little toward providing good news to the Christian living in the prison of mental illness. They backfire pastorally.

How could I, as a Christian, indeed as a theologian of the church, understand anything in my life as though it were separate from God? This is clearly impossible. And yet how could I confess my faith in the God who is "a very present help in trouble" (Ps. 46:1) when I felt entirely abandoned by that God? And if this torture did have something to do with God, was it punishment, wrath, chastisement? Was I, to use a phrase of Jonathan Edwards, simply a "sinner in the hands of an angry God"? What was God doing to me, if it was God's handiwork, and why? Surely the detailed answers to these questions will be as individual for each sufferer of mental illness as is the personal history of each individual and her illness. But these are the questions I wanted to struggle with, partly for my own benefit and partly for the benefit of the body of Christ.

In an age when we have not only the technology but also the ready habit of attempting to medicate the pains of the body, mind, and soul into remission, these questions have become pressing in a new way. There may be remission, but that is all it is. The shadows and pain of human existence cannot be permanently swept away by medication and therapy; those who have more serious mental diseases such as schizophrenia and bipolar disorder will never be able to come off medications as though finally "cured."

As time went on, however, I realized that I could not write such a book as an academic theologian dealing with the problem at an objective distance. This meant, of course, that I had to reveal more of myself than I had wanted. I decided that I needed to be self-revelatory for the purposes of addressing the questions I list above.

What follows, then, is an attempt to allow the reader enough of a glimpse of my questions as they engage my own experience of the darkness that was often my only perceived companion. The central focus of this book, however, as I hope will be apparent, is not my own experience of the pain but a witness to the working of the triune God in the pain of one mentally ill Christian. Here it will be key to focus on the theocentric rather than the anthropocentric, on the triune God rather than on the self. This may sound backwards. But if I were to focus just on myself, this book would be no different from the many that line the shelves of many bookstores, with their personal narratives of illness and recovery.

For the Christian, the focus of life is not properly the self alone as an independent agent; rather, the purpose of the Christian life is "to glorify God and enjoy him forever," as the Westminster Shorter Catechism tells us. We are to seek the voice of the Holy One of Israel and heed his call to the body of Christ for obedience and gratitude. How can one then be obedient in the face of a sometimes severe brain disease? How can one praise the God who made the self when that self is in so much pain so as to wish life extinguished?

I write, then, of my own experience interpreted theologically, with the hope and prayer that this may be of some use to others. It is my way of offering up my own pain to Christ, that it may be redeemed as it touches the lives of others.

> Give to us grace, O Father, not to pass by suffering or joy without eyes to see; give us understanding and sympathy; and guard us from selfishness that we may enter into the joys and sufferings of others; use us to gladden and strengthen those who are weak and suffering; that by our lives we may help others who believe and serve you, and project your light which is the light of life.
>
> H. R. L. Sheppard (1880–1937)

This book is laid out in three parts. In the first part, "Facing Mental Illness," I relate my story and attempt to reach out to others struggling with mental illness. In these first six chapters I deal with issues of mental illness in general and my own experience of the highs and lows of bipolar disorder, narrating some of the hardest episodes of my illness and my hospitalizations. This includes my experience of electroconvulsive therapy.

In the second part, "Faith and Mental Illness," I struggle with specifically theological questions and their bearing on mental illness. In these five chapters, I question the value of the personality and feeling in religious reflection. I also explore the relationship between the brain, mind, and soul, and I discuss the value of prayer for the health of the mentally ill.

In the third and final part, "Living with Mental Illness," I focus on practical issues and advice on how to be a friend to the mentally ill. Since I have used Scripture throughout, a summary of why and how I read Scripture follows these final chapters. I include an appendix which contains a brief checklist of symptoms for those who are attempting to recognize mental illness. It includes the addresses of some websites that may be useful for the reader.

In this second edition, I include an afterword in which I update some of the information on therapies and medications. Of course, I am no doctor, and I imagine that some of this information I have not accurately passed on. New studies and medications have presented new possibilities in the treatment of some of these illnesses, but because I am no authority on this, I will try to guide the reader to sources which are indeed authorities. While my own biographical details are only somewhat updated from the first edition, I also offer some reflections on what I have learned since 2006 as a person who continues to live with a chronic mental illness and a list of suggested questions for group study of the book.

PART ONE

Facing
Mental Illness

1

Darkness

Affliction is the best book in my library.
Martin Luther (1483–1546)

My thirtieth birthday found me as content as the next person, as happy as I had always been, in fact quite unremarkably normal. I was well adjusted, highly productive, married to the man of my dreams, with an active and healthy toddler, beginning to enter successfully my chosen field of study. I understood myself to be mentally quite healthy. I had had a stable and happy childhood, blessed with the benefits too often lacking from many other childhoods. The only exception to the streams-of-mercy-never-ceasing was a somewhat unusual series of tragedies that had struck like waves throughout my youth and young adult years. But even these I had weathered well, or so I had always thought. Looking back now, I see that was not the case.

When I became a mother for the second time, the hem of my mental health began to fray. Motherhood by nature challenges the mental, emotional, spiritual, and physical endurance of any woman. It is a highly over-romanticized and underestimated pressure cooker, matched in potential for the creation of a new family with the destruction of both mother and child. Think—with horror—of the Susan Smiths and Andrea Yateses of the world. Smith drowned her two children in a pond by seat belting them into the car and pushing the car into the water. Yates killed all five of her children, the youngest a newborn, by drowning them one by precious one in the family bathtub. Of course, most postpartum sufferers are not in this dangerous state, nor this detached from reality.

I cannot speak, of course, from experience of the role of the father. I do not mean to discredit his difficulties. I am not aware of the role of the fathers in the Smith and Yates cases. I do know that without the father of my own children, I simply would not have survived thus far. His support and care took the edge off most of my symptoms, especially at this early stage. Without my husband's staunch faithfulness and belief that I would see light beyond this, I simply would not have made it through.

Motherhood, I believe, was only the precipitant for an internal agony that I had been holding back for years. Maybe God had postponed my storm at sea until I could be buoyed by the hopefulness and joy that I derived from my children and husband. The experience as a whole and the experiences that constituted the eventual illness were at the least bewildering and at most terrifying. The blue sky, which normally fills my heart, stung my soul. Beautiful things like oriental rugs and good food like bean soup absolutely exhausted me. Noise was amplified in my ears, and I fled sound and conversation in search of silence. Small tasks became existential problems: how and why to fold the laundry, empty the dishwasher, do the grocery shopping. My memory failed me. I was unable to read or write. And it went downhill from there. A back and forth in and out of darkness lasted for years.

There are many psalms of lament, but Psalm 88 seemed to fit me. It ends in the Book of Common Prayer translation with "Darkness is my only companion." Yes, even some of my friends deserted me, except ones who are now the dearest and truest of friends. I was no fun to be with whatsoever, so why not desert me? "What has got into her? Why is she in such a bad mood? She can't even remember my name!"

I have a chronic disease, a brain disorder that used to be called manic depression and is now called, supposedly less offensively, bipolar disorder. However one tries to soften the blow of the diagnosis, the fact remains that bipolar disorder is a subset of the larger category unhappily called "major mental illnesses." By the latter part of my thirties, I had sought help from several psychiatrists, social workers, and mental health professionals, one a Christian but mostly non-Christians. I had been in active therapy with a succession of therapists over several years and had been introduced to many psychiatric medications, most of which brought quite unpleasant side effects and only a few of which relieved my symptoms to some degree. Those medications that have in fact been helpful, I must say despite my own disinclination toward meds, have been a strand in the cord that God has woven for me as the lifeline cast out in my free fall. The medications have helped me to rebuild some of "myself" so that I can continue to be the kind of mother, priest, and writer that I believe God wants me to be. "A threefold cord is not quickly broken" (Eccles. 4:12). The three cords to my rope were the religious (worship and prayer), the psychological (psychotherapy), and the physical (medical treatments, hospitalization, and exercise).

Yet while therapists and counselors, psychiatrists and medications abound, I found no one to help me make sense of my pain with regard to my life before the triune God. I write this book, then, by way of an offering, as what I wish someone had written to help me make sense of the pain and the apparent incongruity of that agony with the Christian life. Those Christians who have not faced the ravages of mental illness should not be quick with advice to those who do suffer. Platitudes such as "Pray harder," "Let Jesus in," or even "Cast all your anxiety on him, because he cares for you" (1 Pet. 5:7), which of course are all sage pieces of advice in and of themselves, may only make the depressive person hurt more.

This is because depression is not just sadness or sorrow. Depression is not just negative thinking. Depression is not just being "down." It is being cast to the very end of your tether and, quite frankly, feeling as though you are being dropped. Likewise, mania is more than speeding mentally, more than euphoria, more than creative genius at work. The sick individual cannot simply shrug it off, pull out of it, or slow down mentally. While God certainly can pick up the pieces and put them together in a new way, this can happen only if the depressed brain makes it through an episode to see again life among the living. At the time of free fall such a possibility seems absolutely unimaginable. Christians who have not experienced symptoms of mental illnesses—the high of mania, the low of depression, the cognitive mush of schizophrenia, the terror of psychosis—must try to accept that this is the case, even if they cannot understand it.

> I loathe my life;
>> I will give free utterance to my complaint;
>> I will speak in the bitterness of my soul.
> I will say to God, Do not condemn me;
>> let me know why you contend against me.
> Does it seem good to you to oppress,
>> to despise the work of your hands
>> and favor the schemes of the wicked?
>   Job 10:1–3

Job is, of course, the quintessential sufferer in the Bible. He suffers immensely and yet always brings his complaint before God. Even when God seems to have abandoned him, Job continues to pray: "Do not condemn me." Even though he speaks "in the bitterness" of his soul, at least he recognizes that he is a soul, and that despite the suffering, he as a soul is related to God. "Does it seem good to you to oppress, to despise the work of your hands and favor the schemes of the wicked?" Even though God seems to favor the wicked, to whom does Job utter his complaint? God.

> Again I saw that under the sun the race is not to the swift, nor the battle to the strong, nor bread to the wise, nor riches to the intelligent, nor favor to the skillful; but time and chance happen to them all.
>
> Ecclesiastes 9:11

When I asked God why this happened, Ecclesiastes answered, Why not? Time and chance happen to all. Why not this time, this chance, and me?

———

Chopping vegetables for a stir-fry. Baby fussing in the background, three-year-old running his toy truck between my feet. Suddenly I see on the cutting board, in place of celery, the severed fingers of my baby daughter. Neat, clean, bloodless. I blink. They are gone now, the celery has returned, the baby is still fussing, her fingers still attached to her hands where they should be, the truck still rumbling along the kitchen floor. I turn back to fixing dinner as though nothing had happened.

An effective coping mechanism: pretending everything is all right, pretending nothing upsetting has happened. It had served me well for some thirty years. Now the storage area in my soul for all the hurts that had been pretended away is overflowing. I need help. Before what I sloughed off was just psychological pain; now my brain is playing tricks on me. Darkness is my closest companion. I need something, but I don't know what. I don't even know how to tell if or when I need help. I don't know what it means to let myself be helped. I never ask for help, even on the odd occasion when I recognize my need for help. That is the definition of me: strong. But now I don't sleep well, can't eat, can't read (a problem for a graduate student), and draw no pleasure from the little things anymore.

Physical symptoms bother me. I see my general practitioner: must be a sinus infection or the flu, or . . . He runs test after test and concludes from the exam and blood work that there is nothing physically wrong with me. He suggests that I be seen in Mental Hygiene upstairs. I am appalled at the thought, but he convinces me.

"Kathryn, from all of the symptoms you have mentioned and from your answers to my questions, I would say that you are in a major depression and that . . ."

I don't hear the rest. A close friend has just been unsuccessfully treated for depression with electroconvulsive therapy. My father and brother had suffered bouts of depression. But I was the cheery one, the well-adjusted one, the happy face of the family. I try to listen to the doctor above the roaring din of my thoughts scrambling to understand, to piece together the meaning of the incidents I had just recounted to him. How could this be and yet I had not even guessed? What does this mean? My head wails, I cannot hear.

Kay Jamison's book *An Unquiet Mind* tells the story of her lifelong struggle with manic-depressive illness and of her career as a psychiatrist specializing in the treatment of mood disorders. Beyond the narrative framework, though, the book does have a thesis (rather unlike William Styron's *Darkness Visible* or Kathy Crosby's *At the Edge of Darkness*). Jamison's thesis is that love pulls one through the suffering. Sounds sweet, almost trite. The kindnesses of strangers and friends, the acceptance of her disease by those who were able, the love of the men who serially played major roles in her healing: love heals.

Why should this seem trite to me? Shouldn't I see this as an authentic, powerful, and appropriate explanation of what pulls us through? Is it just because I am depressed, or naturally cynical, or a theologian? Maybe all of these. But when one looks at the problem of mental illness from a completely secular perspective, Jamison's implicit thesis (clearly meant to be hopeful and hope-filling) in fact can fill me with more despair than ever. After all, human love can seem particularly unreliable and fleeting. At times it is unattainable, at others inexpressible, and usually for the depressed, human love is unsensed, and indeed nonsense. Of course, for the depressed individual, divine love can be unsensed and nonsense as well. But at least it never fails! "[Love] bears all things, believes all things, hopes all things, endures all things" (1 Cor. 13:7). This is true of divine love, and only thereby derivatively of human love. So "love pulls you through," when it is not tied to the love of God in Christ but to the random kindnesses of people who happen at the moment to be in a better humor than I am, is flat. Yet human love, such as that of my husband, can certainly be a conduit for divine love, even for those who do not recognize love's true source. If it is the love of God that we see in the face of Christ Jesus that is promised to pull us through, a love that bears it out to the edge of doom even for the ugly and unlovable such as we are, then the statement that love heals depression is in fact the only light that shines in the dark tunnel.

This leads me to wonder how people who are depressed and do not have the conviction of God's unconditional love to hold them steady (even when they cannot feel or sense that conviction) can survive depression. Maybe they do not have such a pessimistic (or what I would prefer to call realistic) understanding of human love. But anyhow, I am a Christian, and how will I survive my depression? God, please enable me to survive. I must allow God to touch me through those people who by God's grace are enabled to love beyond mere human capacity. And maybe it is this sort of love to which Jamison refers after all, although she never says so explicitly. Again, the love of my husband is like this, a grace-filled love. I suppose, though, that we should not fail to recognize God's love extended toward us even in the seemingly trite kindnesses of the otherwise potentially unkind. Even in the listening and patient ear of a psychotherapist, yes, even though I am financing the relationship. I must allow for the possibility for God to work through that relationship. I suppose we have to allow for the possibility for God to be active even among those who are not aware of his presence. It doesn't matter whether they know it. God is big enough to handle their potential ignorance.

> Help me, O Lord, to make a true use of all disappointments and calamities in this life, in such a way that they may unite my heart more closely with you. Cause them to separate my affections from worldly things and inspire my soul with more vigor in the pursuit of true happiness.
>
> Susanna Wesley (1669–1742), mother of John and Charles Wesley, and seventeen others, nine of whom did not survive childhood

Why, with my religious convictions about the love and mercy of God, with my belief in the unconditional and free grace of God poured out in Jesus even in spite of my basest longings and actions, why would I not be filled with joy at every moment, eager to greet the day with the love of the Lord? Especially with a new, perfect baby, a little girl, born healthy after some twenty weeks of preterm contractions. I had, from the outside, a happy and comfortable, indeed privileged, childhood: a two-parent family, a stable home, a good education. I was never neglected by my parents and was always given the most basic of material blessings that many of the world's children do not have. Amazing that someone even in that cushioned atmosphere should end up in my position, sometimes struggling on the edge of sanity. One of my psychiatrists once suggested that my symptoms as a twelve-year-old sounded like a depression arising from post-traumatic stress syndrome. This syndrome is frequently associated with soldiers who were traumatized by the atrocities they witnessed and committed in war. How could I have had post-traumatic stress syndrome? As a child and young person I did know many people who committed suicide or died in violent accidents. The symptoms of post-traumatic stress syndrome can look somewhat like those of depression. But still, I read about the woman who, as a child, was the subject of the famous photo, the naked girl engulfed in napalm flames as she ran through the Vietnamese jungle. Now an adult, disfigured and disabled from the burns she sustained, she was able to embrace with her remaining arm the weeping, repentant man who had dropped the bomb that killed her family and maimed her for life. She forgave him. *Forgave him.* She leads a productive life. I lead a productive life too, some of the time, but I never faced the atrocities she did. She does not appear to have post-traumatic stress syndrome. How then could I?

I have been challenged by tragedy, but it was always witnessing the tragedy of others, and even now it is witnessing the tragedy of others that I find absolutely unbearable. It sends me into a complete tailspin. One day recently I saw an old man get hit by an oncoming car as he was walking across the street—the thud of his body against the oncoming car, the sight of him dropping to the ground, then trying pitifully to rise. I was the first to reach him, the one to coax him back to his car as he attempted to walk away, the one to take his keys and sit with him until the ambulance came. I was shaky for the next few days. Witnessing the pain of others is very difficult for me.

I remember the first time I was confronted with death. Other than hearing of grandparents and uncles dying, the first time I was struck with the reality of my own mortality was the week I turned twelve years old. One of my church choir buddies was killed when a tree fell on her in her backyard. She lingered for about a day, but it was clear that she would not pull out of the coma. I don't remember how I felt, but I do remember adopting the habit of crossing off the days on my bedside calendar with a perfect black X after that. I was crossing off the days I had that my friend would no longer have. A strange, undiagnosed illness kept me in bed for about a month sometime after that. I suffered head-splitting pain that made me scream out in the middle of the night. I could not keep food down. I remember spending my days under the covers listening to my purple transistor radio. My psychiatrist decades later suggested that may have been my first episode of depression, but at the time no one ever considered that.

Between middle school and college, more tragedies rolled over me. My science lab partner in eighth grade shot himself with his father's hunting rifle one night in a fit of despair after totaling his father's car. That same year, one of my classmate's older brothers killed himself, leaving a note indicating that he had reached his potential in life and had nothing more to "do," as though life were a board game that he had prematurely won. When I was sixteen, my first "real" date was killed in a motorcycle accident. He lingered for a few days, but his head injuries finally claimed his life. The series continued: the brother of our church youth group leader was killed in a drunk driving accident; my gymnastics teammate ended her own life by diving into an empty pool; a friend from church youth group shot himself with his own hunting rifle; my co-counselor from church camp threw himself off a cliff in Hawaii; and a former student (apparently intentionally) overdosed. Later, during my fifth hospitalization in what was then called Yale Psychiatric Institute, another childhood friend hung herself while on suicide watch in a psychiatric hospital thirty miles away. Throughout the years since the first edition of this book, yet more friends and family have taken their own lives. By now I am almost used to hearing news of suicide, if such a thing can be said. Suicide had become somehow "normal," a seemingly acceptable release from one's inner pain.

But one thing truly terrified me, and that was witnessing my brother's depression. Of course I knew where it could lead. Once when he and I were both home from college one summer, I begged him never to do that, never to take his own life. He refused to promise me. He said he just could not make that promise. Every time he became depressed and would be awake knocking about the house at 3:00 a.m., I would be terrified that he would hurt himself. I found myself wanting to scream out, "Just do it, just get it over with and kill yourself if you are not willing to fight! Don't

prolong our agony and yours if that is how this will end anyway!"
I felt terrible for having such thoughts and feelings.

Yet I did gain some insight from my brother's depression as
well as from my father's. These illnesses helped me learn how
to protect others from my own depression years later. I would
come to push away the self-pity and the blaming of others. I
learned to remind myself of my belief that life is a gift. No matter how I felt about my own life, I refused to give in to suicidal
thoughts and acts, even though I often ruminated wildly about
them. Still, my compassion for my brother was matched only by
this anger toward him. He was clearly suffering, and there was
nothing I could do about it. Or at least that is the way I thought
about it then.

I think that people who have not dealt with such grief, either
first or secondhand, simply do not know what happiness is, what
joy is, because they do not know what the depths of pain can be.
It is like this: you cannot know the import of the cross and resurrection unless you have grasped the weight of sin. All those smiley
people out there who always seem to be on an even keel are either
lying or have no idea what joy can be seen from the underside,
because they have no idea of the truly awful pain life can bring.
As Augustine (354–430) said, the hills drive back the water, but the
valleys are filled by it (Sermon 27). In the valleys of depression, one
can find that "well-watered garden," as Genesis 2 describes Eden,
if one is so blessed. Sometimes even depression can be a blessing,
because one can learn about God through his hiding. That usually only comes afterward, because during depression, as during
the flood, the waters of death cover the face of the earth. As with
Noah, it is only afterward that the dove can return with the olive
leaf in its beak, a sign of blessing. Only after the storm can God
set his bow in the clouds as a sign of the covenant.

> Truly, you are a God who hides himself,
> O God of Israel, the Savior.
> Isaiah 45:15

Even here, Isaiah does not say, "Truly he is a God who hides himself." Isaiah addresses God directly, even in God's apparent absence. He acknowledges that this absent God is still the God of his people and his own God. And Isaiah acknowledges that God is Savior, even in hiding. *Truly, you are a God who hides himself, O God of Israel, the Savior.*

During a depression, as during Noah's flood, the good providence of God is hidden from view. All I can see is the storm, all I can smell is the dung of my own ark, and all I can perceive is the very wrath of God. And worse than Noah, I have no companions in my ark, just my own stinky, contentious inner beasts. Darkness is my only companion.

> O blessed Jesus, you know the impurity of our affection, the narrowness of our sympathy, and the coldness of our love; take possession of our souls and fill our minds with the image of yourself; break the stubbornness of our selfish wills and mold us in the likeness of your unchanging love, O you who alone can do this, our Savior, our Lord and our God.
>
> William Temple (1881–1944)

Mental illnesses can present themselves differently from person to person. People with the same diagnosis may have very different symptoms. Some can't get out of bed; some can't sleep. Some eat too much; some can't bring themselves to eat at all. So the diseases are not the symptoms. It is not like cancer, where there is hope at least of cutting out afflicted parts of the body in hopes of eradicating the disease. In mental illnesses, the symptoms plague the whole body and mind equally.

I am not necessarily sad when I am depressed. I am not necessarily "down." Sometimes I just have a gnawing, overwhelming sense of grief, with no identifiable cause. I grieve as though my loved ones were dead. I imagine their funerals. I feel completely alone and isolated. I feel as if I am walking barefoot on broken glass. When one steps on broken glass, the weight of one's body grinds the glass shards in further with every movement. The weight of my very existing grinds the shards of grief deeper into my soul. When I am depressed, every thought, every breath, every conscious moment hurts.

So what do I do? I try to distract myself. Enduring episodes of depression requires that I expend huge amounts of energy just to distract myself. My work, when I can by sheer force of will overcome the depression enough to engage in work, is solace. Prayer, when I can climb out of the hole into which depression throws me, helps momentarily. Of course, theologically speaking, I know it helps more than just momentarily, but that is not the way it feels. Sleeping, while I am sleeping, if I can sleep, helps as an escape. Tasks, busyness, gardening, tidying up: distractions. Mustn't think, mustn't be conscious, mustn't reflect. This escape from consciousness is at the heart of suicidal energy. It is *not* wanting to hurt the self. It is simply wanting *not to hurt*. When I am depressed, it seems that the only way not to hurt is to cease being a center of consciousness.

Distracting myself, though, is itself distressing, because I end up feeling that my every action and thought is a futile attempt to flee from pain that will never ease. Of course, I am not always depressed; in fact, usually I am no longer depressed at all. But when I am, there is no "other side," no perspective, no reminding myself that this will pass . . . yes, of course I remind myself of this, but it only enters the top of my brain and then flits right out again. It is never a "sure and certain knowledge" as John Calvin says of faith.

Other than my childhood episode with what now has been suggested to have been depression, my first real head-on toss into the pit as an adult was, as I have said, after our daughter was born in 1992. Postpartum depression is not pretty. It is tragic. Every instinct in the mother normally pushes toward preserving the life of the child. A healthy mother would give her own life to protect her babies. But in a postpartum depression, reality is so bent that this instinct is blocked. Lack of sleep could alone make anyone depressed and hallucinatory, but on top of that the new mother has a rush of hormones playing havoc with body and brain. Perfectly good mothers have their confidence shaken by the thoughts and feelings they endure in postpartum depression.

I realize now that after our son was born in 1989 I also was not well, but at the time I was under so much stress that I just did not attribute my ill health to anything except to having entered a doctoral program with a two-and-a-half-month preemie slung across my front. Two months of bed rest for preterm labor prior to his birth and subsequent hospitalizations because of his health complications had left me shocked, dazed, and wrung out. And looking back even further, I can remember times in college when I couldn't get out of bed, when I was incredibly irritable for weeks at a time, and when my friends were strained beyond their capacity to bend with my brain chemistry.

Now, by the grace of God and help from psychotherapy and medicine, I have learned how to protect those around me from my depressive episodes and to prevent the shadows from damaging my relationships with family and friends. Some people who suffer use their illnesses as permission to lash out at loved ones. Some disown family and friends, either by running away or by severing relationships. Divorce is a ready exit from either side of the marriage when a partner is mentally ill. Especially in the case of bipolar sufferers, manic episodes with their potential impetuous affairs and drastic overspending can ruin marriages. Some abuse their family verbally or physically, blaming them for their own sufferings. I thank God that I never was subject to any of this. When I was hypomanic, my therapist kept a tight rein on me, seeing me every day if needed. The same was true when I was suicidally depressed. She even accepted phone calls in her off hours and figuratively held my hand through many a rough time.

My method of dealing with bipolar energies was to dance with my daughter, who would look at me with unbelieving delight, surprised to find a happy mommy. I would garden. I would play the piano and sing at the top of my lungs all the show tunes I knew. This could get rather annoying to my family. I worked hard to avoid stores and thus the temptation to overspend. But being disciplined with oneself during this stage is very difficult; mania is almost defined by lack of discipline.

My method of dealing with depression was not to lash out but to retreat. When I was depressed, I would curl up on our bed and sleep. I could sleep at any time of the day or night, and sleep soundly for hours. I would avoid the family, in part because the noise was so painful to me that I could not stand it and in part because I did not want to make them miserable by my presence. I did not understand at that time that my family and friends truly missed me. I later came to realize this and moved my nest from our bed to the living room as I improved. I was silent and still unable to move, but at least I was there with the children and my husband.

This leads me to a warning about the children of people who live with mental illnesses. Most children are very sensitive and perceptive; they understand much more than we give them credit for. Parents should explain to their children what the nature of the problem is, or the children may create scenarios in their minds that are worse than the realities of the situation. They may even blame themselves. Our children pretended they were comfortable with Mommy's spiritual, psychological, and physical absences behind the door of the bedroom, but they became absolutely unhinged when I went into the hospital. Grades slipped, moods dropped. Our son became more aggressive, and our daughter withdrew. My husband and I were so embarrassed at the hospitalization that we did not even tell teachers at the children's schools. This was a big mistake that at the time we did not recognize.

We had not prepared the children well enough for my first hospital stay and did not share the details with them. Children need communication at times even as horrible as these, but it must be judicious communication. Do not mention suicidal thoughts or gestures. Just something simple. "Mommy is sick. She is very sad. She needs to go to the hospital. She will get better and be home soon. The doctors will take good care of her." Even telling children that "Mommy has a brain disorder" is better than saying nothing, or than saying that her heart hurts. Children have heard about heart attacks and know how serious they are. Don't bring in half-truths for the sake of protecting the children. Speak matter-of-factly, quietly, calmly. Stress that the hospital is a good place for those who are sick. Tell them that it is no one's fault and that the doctors are doing their job and will take good care of Mommy.

When the children did come for a visit to the hospital, they became entirely unglued. They didn't like seeing people catatonic, jumpy, uncontrollable, nor did they like seeing me in such a pale state. They refused to return to visit me in the hospital. Of course I thoroughly understood. I didn't want to be there either. Even though my husband had tried to make the whole situation positive by promising Happy Meals afterward, that first visit was not much of a success. However, the children and I did get to cuddle on the couch, which was very reassuring for all of us. Once again I could be Mommy, even at such a low energy point, and they could be children who weren't expected to suck it up for the sake of the outside world.

So family is very important. The support of a loving spouse is very comforting. My husband, Matthew, is the most loving and most patient partner I could ever imagine. I could never have asked for more. I would question how he was putting up with this blob of a wife, or with the zippy version, with no in-betweens. The chores of the household fell on him: laundry, cooking, shopping, child minding. And he still had a full-time job, which he had to cut back. He is a helpmate given by the grace of God. I shudder to think what I would have done without his support and encouragement. Maybe my suicidal urges would have become reality: in many ways I owe my life to my husband.

My mother came to stay with the children and to help run the household while I was in the hospital. I don't remember how long she was with us, but it was not a short stint. She bore the yeoman's burden while I was in the hospital, trying to relieve my husband of the cooking and cleaning and ferrying the children to and from school. This allowed Matthew to return to work and kept the children on a fairly even keel. I don't even remember any more than this, because that time is still fuzzy in my memory, and according to my psychiatrist, it will always be. Some things I remember quite clearly, and others I cannot recall at all. That is probably a mercy.

Friendship also is so important for people who live with mental illnesses. I think I might not have crashed so hard after our daughter's birth if one of my closest friendships had remained a support in my life. A host of factors, including the symptoms of my depression, tested her beyond the point of her ability to love me. Having that support knocked out from under me was a blow that I could not absorb at the time. In depression, it is as though you lack shock absorbers for the potholes and you bottom out easily when you hit them. Friendship is very important for those with poor mental health, but it is *very* hard to be a true friend to someone in such a condition. It is just too difficult for some people and for some relationships.

> Even my best friend, whom I trusted,
> who broke bread with me,
>   has lifted up her heel and turned against me.
>   Psalm 41:9

One way to help your friends understand is, as with children, to explain calmly and objectively your diagnosis. I told my friend of my illness only years later. How could she want to be associated with such a groaning blob as I? If I had told her why I was in such a state, I imagine now that she would not have been so impatient with me, but at the time I felt so alone I could not even reach out. I am not advocating telling everyone you know that you are ill. This is a challenge to handle as you see fit in your own life. But those who are closest to you should be warned that your behavior may be different from usual and will be for a while, until the medicines get sorted out. They may even be able to help you with feedback. Tell your friends when you are on a new medicine, and ask them to let you know how you seem after a few weeks. Do you seem outwardly peppier, with more energy, less grumpy?

Sometimes a person with a mental illness is capable only of being on the receiving end of friendship. Yet it can for this reason be extremely difficult to be the friend of someone with these kinds of illnesses. It can be boring to be with a person who has no conversation to make, no desire to go out with you, eat with you, talk to you. And someone who is so little fun to be with can worry you, annoy you, overwhelm you.

How can friends show their support, then? Personally, I hated having people ask me how I felt, because I was trying very hard to be OK and didn't want anyone noticing that I was not well. This is, however, not the case for everyone. Reaching out to a person with a mental illness will at least be appreciated as a token of friendship and concern. One suggestion is simply to ask your friend how you can help. What can you do? The most helpful things for me were offers to bring meals, do laundry, watch the children. Even though I often did not accept these offers because of a misplaced sense of pride, which depression can foster, knowing that someone cared enough to offer was a source of encouragement.

The friends who were present in their concern but did not demand anything of me were helpful. This meant sometimes my not communicating for weeks or months, when I was incapable of conversation. During my hospitalizations, I generally asked friends not to visit. I was too embarrassed. I think I would approach this differently were I to be hospitalized again. It might have lessened the monotony for me and also might have helped my friends not to worry so much.

But frankly, I wondered throughout the time whether I had any friends at all. This was not because of my friends but because of the nature of my illness. While in hypomania (a less dramatic and dangerous form of mania), I felt that everyone loved me and found me scintillating; indeed I found myself scintillating. However, in depression I could not imagine that anyone could really love me, want to be there for me, find me still worthy of friendship.

Truly darkness seemed my only companion. Of this I was quite convinced.

One very important way to help your friends who suffer from mental illnesses is to pray for them. The assurance that people were praying for me, since I had so much trouble praying for myself, was indeed a balm in Gilead. My true friends during this time were the ones I knew were praying for me. It can be very difficult to pray for someone day in and day out, over and over again, especially when you see little improvement, when you feel like a scratched CD uttering the same phrases over and over, like the woman who pounded and pounded on the door of the judge: "Grant me justice against my opponent" (Luke 18:3). Even so, this was so vital for me. I do not mean to say that the *idea* of people praying for me was a great comfort, although I do suppose this is true to an extent. I mean the *fact* that people were praying for me was key in my dealing with my illness. In other words, it is not just that I was touched that people would think of me. Prayer is more than merely thinking of someone, even though it does involve thought. My point here is that I believe in the efficacy of prayer, in God's pleasure at hearing our desires and needs and in providing for that which we seek in prayer. That many people were knocking on God's door for me strengthened me in my putting up with the disease and sped the healing, even though the full healing was not an immediate reality. Maybe a degree of healing would never have come if people had not been praying.

2

Mental Illness

Jesus did not come to remove suffering
or to explain it away.
He came to fill it with His presence.

Paul Claudel (1868–1955)

The mentally ill are one of the groups of handicapped people
against whom it still seems to be socially acceptable to hold prejudice. Despite the Jane Pauleys, the Brooke Shieldses, the Kay Redfield Jamisons, and other well-known folks who have experienced
some form of mental illness, this prejudice seems to be as real
in Christian communities as in the secular world. Why is this? I
would suggest that Christian communities still have a fear of the
mentally ill. In part we do not understand mental illnesses. In part
there is a false assumption that the Christian life should always be
an easy path. In part the problem of suffering is hard to grasp. In
The Problem of Pain, C. S. Lewis suggests that suffering is uniquely
difficult for the Christian, the one who believes in a good God.
If there were no good God to factor into the equation, suffering

would still be painful as an experience but ultimately meaningless because random. For the Christian, who believes in the crucified and risen Messiah, suffering is always meaningful. It is meaningful because of the One in whose suffering we participate. This is not to say, of course, that suffering will be pleasant nor that it is to be sought. Rather, the personal suffering of the Christian finds a correlate in Christ's suffering, which gathers up our tears, calms our sorrows, and points us toward Christ's resurrection.

According to the National Mental Health Advisory Council study of 1993, 2.8 percent of the adult population of the United States at that time, or approximately 5.6 million Americans, suffered from severe and persistent mental illness.[1] A quarter of a million homeless people and 200,000 incarcerated people suffered from mental illness at that time. In addition, the National Mental Health Advisory Council estimated that 7–9 million children were suffering from or were at risk for severe, long-term mental illness. According to a National Institute for Mental Health study, 22.1 percent of all adults in any particular year suffer from a diagnosable psychiatric disorder.

Take the 5.6 million with severe disorders, and multiply this by 2.1 (this is the figure the government uses for the average number of other adults in the average-size family). Add these 11.8 million persons to the 5.6 million, and

> we see that at the least nearly 17 million Americans are directly affected, in their nuclear families alone, by persistent and serious forms of mental illness. [In addition,] lifetime prevalence rates of psychiatric disorders were estimated to be between 28.8 and 38 percent. The numbers only confirm what most of us already know: that individuals with serious mental illness are *everywhere*—among us, with us, all around us—and are a lot closer to home than we usually care to acknowledge.[2]

As of 1999, government estimates of the costs of mental illness were well over $200 billion: costs from loss of productivity, lost earnings caused by premature death, and law enforcement.

The three most significant and serious mental illnesses affecting these mentally ill, known as Major Mental Illnesses, are major depression, bipolar disorder, and schizophrenia. Painting in broad strokes, we can say that all of these are marked by lows and/or highs of energy and pleasure; sleep disturbances; weight gain and/or loss; cognitive and creative blunting and/or sharpening. Major depression is often marked by a loss of interest in all aspects of life, even those that normally would cause pleasure, and a presence of excruciating psychic and even physical pain. Bipolar disorder involves cycling back and forth between these painful lows and exhilarating or fearsome highs with a dramatic bungee-like effect that is never thrilling. It's more like an ordinary tennis ball bouncing from floor to ceiling and back again. Schizophrenia includes "positive" symptoms (that is, symptoms that are "added on" to usual experience) and "negative" symptoms (diminishment of usual function). The positive symptoms may include delusions, visions, auditory experiences, and paranoia. The negative symptoms may include dulled cognition and impaired ability to handle the most basic tasks of daily life. Some of these symptoms may also be present in bipolar disorder. When schizophrenia includes symptoms of depression and/or bipolar disorder, it is called schizoaffective disorder.

How then does one become mentally ill and come to exhibit these sorts of symptoms? There are many theories, but the reigning ones suggest that the cause is a combination of nature and nurture, that is, one's brain biology or genetic makeup combined with the stresses and traumas of one's past and present life and social context. This means that strategies for combating mental illness will usually combine both psychotherapeutic and medical approaches.

Just one of the therapies used is interpersonal therapy. Many types of therapies come under this category. Cognitive behavioral therapy is one of these which attempts to retrain thought processes to be more productive and less maladaptive. Psychoanalysis tends to be used less frequently these days as a treatment especially for schizophrenia, although insights from the theory can still be used even there. It also may be used in the treatment of depression and bipolar disorder.[3]

Medical therapies include four general classes of antidepressant medications.[4] The SSRIs, or serotonin selective reuptake inhibitors, such as Prozac, Paxil, Luvox, Zoloft, and Celexa, are among the most popular. They boost levels of serotonin in the brain. Tricyclics, such as Elavil, Anafranil, Norpramin, Tofranil, and Pamelor, affect both serotonin and dopamine in the brain. The MAOIs, or monoamine oxidase inhibitors, prevent the breakdown of serotonin, dopamine, and norepinephrine. Among these are Nardil and Parnate. This class is among the most dangerous of the four classes of medications because of the medications' potential side effects, which can be triggered in conjunction with common foods such as cheese, chocolate, red wine, soy sauce, and any other fermented products. Atypical antidepressants, which operate on multiple neurotransmitter symptoms, are Asendin, Wellbutrin, Seroquel, and Effexor. In addition, sometimes other medications are used in conjunction with antidepressants—for example, antianxiety drugs like BuSpar, and benzodiazepines such as Valium, Ativan, Clonapin, and Xanax; antipsychotics such as Haldol, Risperdol, Zyprexa, and Geodon; and mood stabilizers such as Lithium, Tegretol, Lamictal, and Depakote. Another treatment for the Major Mental Illnesses is electroconvulsive therapy, or ECT, which will be described in a later chapter.

What does mental illness actually look like and feel like? How is depression different from just feeling sad or discouraged or blue? I am not the only one, certainly, to try to describe it. In his award-winning book *Darkness Visible*, William Styron writes,

> The pain is unrelenting, and what makes the condition intolerable is the foreknowledge that no remedy will come—not in a day, an hour, a month, or a minute. If there is mild relief, one knows that it is only temporary; more pain will follow. It is hopelessness even more than pain that crushes the soul. So the decision-making of

daily life involves not, as in normal affairs, shifting from one annoying situation to another less annoying—or from discomfort to relative comfort, or from boredom to activity—but moving from pain to pain. One does not abandon, even briefly, one's bed of nails, but is attached to it wherever one goes.[5]

Here is another first-person account by Andrew Solomon from his book *The Noonday Demon*, in which he describes one of his episodes of depression. Notice the role of sleep and sleep disturbance here. These complications are typical of the symptoms of the Major Mental Illnesses.

I did not sleep much that night, and I could not get up the following day. . . . I lay very still and thought about speaking, trying to figure out how to do it. I moved my tongue but there were no sounds. I had forgotten how to talk. I began to cry, but there were no tears, only a heaving incoherence. I was on my back. I wanted to turn over, but I couldn't remember how to do that either. I tried to think about it, but the task seemed colossal. I thought that perhaps I'd had a stroke, and then I cried again for a while. At about three o'clock that afternoon, I managed to get out of bed and go to the bathroom. I returned to the bed shivering.[6]

I myself remember being unable to get out of bed even to use the bathroom—being in pain because the need was so great, but still unable to move. Sometimes I would wait so long that the need would lessen as I became dehydrated throughout the course of the day.

Leonard Wolff, the husband of noted author Virginia Wolff, kept a diary in which he tells of the illnesses that plagued her throughout her life. His account points out especially how people with Major Depression can be challenging to care for, and how it may take much patience and energy to keep them physically healthy.

If left to herself, she would have eaten nothing at all and would have gradually starved herself to death. It was extraordinarily difficult ever to get her to eat enough to keep her strong and well. . . . In

the early acute, suicidal stage of the depression, she would sit for
hours overwhelmed with hopeless melancholia, silent, making no
response to anything said to her. When the time came for a meal,
she would pay no attention whatsoever to the plate of food put
before her. I could usually induce her to eat a certain amount, but
it was a terrible process. Every meal took an hour or two; I had
to sit by her side, put a spoon or fork in her hand, and every now
and again ask her very quietly to eat and at the same time touch
her arm or hand. Every five minutes or so she might automatically
eat a spoonful.[7]

Once I was out to lunch with a friend who knew I was sick and
was making his best efforts to get me to eat my soup. "You're not
eating. Does it just not taste good?"

"Yes," I responded, "I am eating it." The soup remained in the
bowl, and I went home feeling full.

Swiss psychiatrist Eugen Bleuler, who coined the term *schizophrenia*, linked mania to artistic production, and Kay Redfield
Jamison follows suit in her book *Touched with Fire*. When one
is in a depressed state, creative production is nearly impossible,
but in even a relatively mild hypomanic state, if the person has a
talent to begin with, prodigious creation can be achieved. Bleuler
describes the thinking of the manic patient: "The *thinking* of the
manic is flighty. He jumps by-paths from one subject to another,
and cannot adhere to anything. With this the ideas run along
very easily and involuntarily, even so freely that it may be felt as
unpleasant by the patient."[8]

The grandiosity of the manic mind is suggested by Edgar
Allan Poe, himself apparently afflicted with bipolar disorder. While
the depressed mind is flat, lacking energy, the hypomanic mind
images itself as captivating, glorious, resplendent. Poe questions
how much this state is actually positively related to his genius and
ability to write.

I am come of a race noted for vigor of fancy and ardor of passion.
Men have called me mad; but the question is not yet settled, whether

madness is or is not the loftiest intelligence—whether much that is glorious—whether all that is profound—does not spring from disease of thought—from moods of mind exalted at the expense of the general intellect.[9]

Symptoms of schizophrenia are described in the following anecdote from *The Autobiography of a Schizophrenic Girl*. Notice that they include both hallucinations and auditory experiences, and the girl's divorce from reality is apparent. The remarkable thing about this book is that the author, Renée, reached a healthy enough state to relate her own schizophrenic experiences, a rare state for people with such a severe disease as this.

> One day, while I was in the principal's office, suddenly the room became enormous, illuminated by a dreadful electric light that cast false shadows. Everything was exact, smooth, artificial, extremely tense; the chairs and tables seemed models placed here and there. Pupils and teachers were puppets revolving without cause, without objective. I recognized nothing, nobody. It was as though reality, attenuated, had slipped away from all these things and these people. Profound dread overwhelmed me, and as though lost, I looked around desperately for help. I heard people talking but I did not grasp the meaning of the words. The voices were metallic, without warmth or color.[10]

While genetics bears a strong influence on a person's developing mental illness, I must emphasize that biology is not destiny. Yes, mental illnesses may run in families. As I have said, my brother and father both suffered from depressions. One of my first cousins made an uncompleted attempt on his life, and two others completed suicide. On the other side of the family, a great-grandfather was an alcoholic. Sometimes alcoholics suffer from mental illness and use alcohol to self-medicate. Our family tree holds stories of "eccentrics." Whether or not they would have been diagnosed today is of course unclear, but they seem to have exhibited symptoms.

It is generally assumed that stress can cause genetic predispositions to mental illness to spill over into actual symptoms. This is clearly the case with the stress of postpartum depression. Not every mother responds negatively to the stress of the postpartum period. It is assumed that those who are predisposed to this depression may end up developing the illness when put under the psychic and physical stress of pregnancy, delivery, and infant care.[11] However, not everyone with a family history of mental illness develops the symptoms, and not everyone with mental illness has a family history.

So it is clear that most cases of mental illness are a combination of nature and nurture, of brain chemistry and life stress. This would suggest that we need to protect our mental health as we do our physical health. If mental illness is not only genetically coded but also stress-related, we would do well to be careful of the stressors we take on. This would mean, among other things, impressing upon our youth the dangers of street drugs and alcohol abuse. It would mean taking greater vigilance of our health when we go through stressful times in our lives. It would mean making more ready use of mental health therapists for our psychological well-being, as well as seeking the spiritual guidance of clergy.

3

Temptation to Suicide

I loathe my life.

Job 10:1

According to Kay Jamison Redfield, suicide is the third leading
cause of death for nineteen- to twenty-four-year-olds. Globally, she
says, it kills over one million per year. This makes it seem as though
suicide must be an attractive alternative to some. Why should one
not commit suicide? The answers apparently are obvious to the sane
of mind. Why would anyone want to do such a thing? The desire
for self-protection is built in to the healthy human mind. Suicidal
desire is, of course, one of the factors that define the frontier between illness and health. Self-protection is healthy and "normal,"
while the urge to end one's life is unhealthy and "abnormal."

> Not only is suicide a sin, it is the sin. It is the ultimate and absolute
> evil, the refusal to take an interest in existence; the refusal to take
> the oath of loyalty to life. The man who kills a man, kills a man.
> The man who kills himself, kills all men; as far as he is concerned
> he wipes out the whole world.
>
> G. K. Chesterton (1874–1936)

Chesterton's view here is typical of a Christian assessment of suicide: it is a sin, even the gravest of sins. At the same time, plenty of Christians commit this grave sin. Suicide may be the ultimate act of those suffering illnesses, whether mental illnesses or any other debilitating disorder. I cannot imagine someone killing herself unless she were sick, physically or mentally. I hear that it is estimated that in 90 percent of suicides the person suffers from mental illness. That seems to me a very small percentage.

I used to think that suicide was the most selfish act imaginable. It leaves family, friends, and colleagues in terrible grief. I have witnessed far too many who have been left behind by the suicides of loved ones. Even one such grieving family is one too many. And now that I myself understand what it means to be plagued by suicidal thoughts, I think differently about those who have taken their own lives. I now think that suicide is the most pitiful act. I am no longer angry with my friends who took their lives. I feel nothing now for them except compassion, pain, and sorrow. Suicide is an act that of course is to be rejected at all costs. It is an option only as a non-option. But now I understand that the one who takes her own life is in horrifying agony. Instead of being angry at the suicide, I now have pity.

And yet suicide is indeed an ultimately selfish act. When one is plagued by suicidal urges, one can feel completely isolated and imprisoned within the self. There is no outside the self. At that point, relieving oneself of one's own life may seem like the only escape route, the only way beyond the suffering. The act of suicide is selfish insofar one is curved in on oneself, locked within the prison of psychic pain. There is nothing but the "I" in pain. And I suppose that is a sort of selfishness. But as far as I can tell, this is not a consciously wrought "selfish" act. Although I would imagine that not all suicides are alike.

While I was sick, I experienced much suicidal thinking and wishing. This in itself distressed me, because I as a Christian believe that life is a gift from God. It is to be lived to the glory of God. How ungrateful was I that I would want to return it to the Giver? But it was a gift I no longer wanted from a lover I no longer knew.

Trucks bearing down on me as I look to cross the street: eerily inviting. Especially the square-front, flat-nosed eighteen-wheeler. Such a comforting sight. I imagine myself stepping out in front of it as it barrels down the road. Blessed relief.

Counting pills. Do I have enough to settle the matter without landing in the hospital emergency room? I either have to do it not at all, or have to do it so well that I don't end up half-alive in the hospital, or worse, permanently disabled.

> A bruised reed He will not break,
>   and a dimly burning wick he will not quench.
> Isaiah 42:3

I am indeed a bruised reed, a dimly burning wick. How did I get this depressed? Collecting, hoarding, storing away one by precious one the pills that are supposed to help my brain. Pills that will relieve me finally from my misery. Imagining: practicing on my wrists. Razor's edge, cool, clean, and sharp, entering the skin I can no longer feel. Curiosity: blood. At least I would know that I am indeed alive. Wrong and right: desire for death and yet for life. How did I get this mad?

> Your hurt is incurable,
>   your wound is grievous.
> There is none to uphold your cause,
>   no medicine for your wound,
>   no healing for you.
> Jeremiah 30:12–13

Visit this place, O Lord, and drive far from it all snares of the enemy; let your holy angels dwell with us to preserve us in peace;

and let your blessing be upon us always; through Jesus Christ our
Lord. Amen.

Book of Common Prayer, 140

How can I even think these thoughts? My children, good God,
my children. I cannot do this to them, to my husband, to my family. Dear God, hold me through this. I must not, cannot, will not
act on this. But I want it so badly sometimes that I shake, I panic,
I pace. I must not, must not, must not.

⁓

"Promise me, Kathryn, that you will call me whenever you feel
you are in danger. Promise me. You may not leave my office until
you promise me." My therapist was faithful beyond measure.

⁓

I heard on National Public Radio the other day that a man in
France withdrew his life savings from the bank, the equivalent of
twenty-six thousand dollars, and set it on fire in his bathtub. Then
he took a bottle of sleeping pills. He was rescued and put into a
psychiatric hospital. He now wonders why he did it. I have never
been that destructive, thank God. But seeing and hearing things
that weren't there made me feel truly crazy. For some reason the
garbled, mixed voices, as if at a fuzzy cocktail party, came to me
while I was in the kitchen, and rarely elsewhere. I was so depressed
that my mind was bent and broken.

⁓

What does suicide mean for the Christian? It is still official Roman
Catholic teaching that suicides may not be buried in consecrated
ground. This is in part to serve as a deterrent. Suicide itself is not
technically considered one of the seven deadly sins. But as a form
of murder, suicide is unforgivable. The offense is so great, and the
nature of the crime is such that it leaves no possibility for repentance
and reconciliation. The Christian understands the body to be the

temple of the Holy Spirit. "Do you not know . . . that you are not your own? For you were bought with a price; therefore glorify God in your body" (1 Cor. 6:19–20). Glorify God in your physical body; glorify God in the body of Christ, the community of the faithful. Life is something for which Christians are bound to give thanks.

Certainly I do not want to be heard as advocating suicide. For all my suicidal thinking, I *knew* what I believed in the deepest pit: even though I could not feel it, I knew that suicide is objectively wrong. In any case, how do we respond pastorally to the case of the suicide? Can we say that God does not forgive even here? Do we refuse to officiate at or to attend the funeral of a suicide?

Nicholas Wolterstorff's moving book *Lament for a Son* recounts the tragic death of his son in a mountain-climbing accident. In a passage where Wolterstorff tries to describe his agony at the loss of his own son, he makes the following comment about the suicide of a friend's son.

> The son of a friend—same age as Eric—died a few weeks before Eric. The friend's son committed suicide. The pain of his life was so intense that he took the life that gave the pain. I thought for a time that such a death must be easier to bear than the death of one with zest for life. He wanted to die. When I talked to the father, I saw that I was wrong.[1]

That comment has haunted me. It betrays a common misperception that suicides want to die. I am convinced that this is not the case. Wolterstorff did not understand that the pain left by the suicide of a loved one is of a different order from even the tragic loss and agony that he and his wife experienced at the death of their son. His comment, even while followed by the statement that he realized his mistake, shows how little we grasp the pain that families bear in the wake of a suicide. The world does not understand what it means to struggle with the temptation to suicide, to bear the legacy of a suicide attempt, to lose someone to suicide, to live with the loss, guilt, and shame. I wish we all could live in such a happy land where these did not exist.

Suicide usually leaves in its wake family and friends who in the midst of the horrendous pain grope for meaning, for comprehension of the deed. These family and friends present a case for delicate and loving pastoral care from the church. In fact, this type of pastoral care is different from pastoral care in any other kind of loss. At the risk of putting too sharp a point on it here, no loss of a loved one can ever be as painful as when it is by suicide. Not only is there the normal grief of the death of a loved one, but there is also the pain of having to face the fact that the loved one was in such agony as to take her own life. The despair of those who are left with the legacy of their loved one's final act is next to impossible to bear. The guilt, the shame, the fear that another loved one may follow suit: these are simply beyond imagination to us who have not been there. Our pastoral care will be challenged. We must witness to the love of God in a different and more challenging way.

And what of pastoral care for parishioners who are suicidal?[2] Provided that we are aware of the gravity of the situation, how do we help and support and encourage such persons not to act on their despair? I cannot stress enough: refer, refer, refer to professional psychiatric care. We ourselves can urge that they borrow from the faith of their brothers and sisters in Christ. Encourage regular worship, daily if possible, and not only in the privacy of personal prayer and devotion. Even there, maybe especially there, the devil will be waiting, subtly turning them back in on themselves and away from God. Provide the possibility for worship in communion with other brothers and sisters in Christ. If praying and praising are impossible for the time being for them, which they may well be, offer the prayer and praise of the community of faith. Urge them to clothe themselves in the faith of the saints, and point them to the prayers of the great cloud of witnesses. Encourage them not to be ashamed or afraid to rest on the saints' devotion if they can muster none of their own. Help them to lean on the body of Christ. Remind them that the good news is that they are *not* their own. Assure them that they are not *on* their own. Follow through to make this a reality. Remind them that if they cannot praise right now, that circumstance will change. Provide opportunities for the body of Christ to pray for and with them. This may mean building into the week additional times for corporate worship and prayer. Help them to remember the hope of the gospel, even if they cannot access it intellectually or emotionally, or find relief in it. Remind them that it is the act and not the feeling that matters right now in their lives before God. Gently but firmly tell them not to act on feelings of despair.

I do think a Christian's suicide is the final act of disobedience, of betrayal of the Creator. Of course, I know this is often not consciously chosen, or when it is conscious, it is a choice born of tremendously unbearable pain. A friend's pastor suffocated himself in a plastic garbage bag, leaving the whole congregation asking questions such as, "What could we have done? What should we have done?" If they had noticed the symptoms, maybe they could have confronted him and begged that he get help, reassuring him that they were all with him. It may have been that they could have done nothing to help him, but research on the survival rates of uncompleted suicides points in the opposite direction. There is almost always something we can do. This pastor's death shook the congregation so, more than if he had been simply their boss or business partner. This was the man who had offered the gospel, who had preached words of hope. Yet he committed the ultimate act of hopelessness.

The stakes are high: the Christian's suicide in effect contradicts every good word about God one could ever have preached, undoes every good work dedicated to God and neighbor that one could have accomplished. I must not allow myself so to undermine my life's vocation. I pray to God for strength to hold on. Lord, have mercy.

4

Mania

Mania is sickness for one's friends, depression for
one's self.

Robert Lowell (1917–77)[1]

Dear God what is happening to me I can't even speak. My mind
races races zooms phrases run together ideas bleed what is happening calm down just calm down you are exaggerating. I believe, Lord;
help my unbelief. Nothing is wrong. Nothing is wrong. Nothing
nothing is wrong. Why is the doorbell ringing ringing who is here
dear God who is coming for me who is going to think I am crazy
even though I am fine just fine if only my mind would stop racing
I am *not* going to any hospital why would Matthew have called
them and not told me? You are paranoid. Stop it. Stop it. Stop.
No one wants to take you to the hospital. Just Matthew's friend
coming over. Paranoia is nothing more than excessive narcissism.
Unattractive, unchristian. Why are my teeth chattering why am I
hyperventilating I am not cold. Dance. Go dance.

Snowstorm. Gorgeous exotic turbulent swirls of snow. Magic. The world tingles. My brain sparkles. All things connect.

Panic. Am breathing too fast, am going to choke, am going to lose my vision. I feel drunk but have had no drink. I watch myself move, listen to myself speak as though to another. What will she say? How does her mouth move? What will she do? Panic help someone help me.

Have never found the condiments aisle so fascinating. Never even really thought about condiments: pickles, relishes, sauces. Who would want a vinegared vegetable, after all, when one could have it fresh? But look at all these pickles. Sweet sour dill kosher (how kosher are they really?) peppers onions cauliflowers even eggs baby gherkins slices chunks relishes spreads green red white orange brown all because long ago before refrigeration our papas and mamas had to find a way to preserve the crop for the lean winter months. Of course that is how cheese came to be too, because when you have too much milk but no fridge you get a stinky mess unless you make cheese which itself is a stinky mess but more edible than soured milk, according to most cheese eaters that is. Jars jars jars of pickles.

What was that? Calling my name? Are they coming for me? Am taking too long in the pickle aisle . . . talking to the jars? . . . everybody must be watching . . . someone must have called the manager . . . Oh good they are calling someone else's name . . . but what if that is a tactic to calm me down so then they can pounce on me before I try to run away . . . clever, clever . . . don't be paranoid, the height of narcissism . . . but what if I am right?

Delicious, exhilarating, a rush. I walk six inches off the ground. If I just go a bit faster and jump I will fly.

Hypomania can be fun at first, but if one goes too high or too fast, the fun ends and the nightmare begins.

What am I doing here in the car? How did I get here? I don't remember driving here. Tears. Breathing too fast again. Should call for help. Calm down. Why do I keep telling myself to calm down? Jesus, where are you? Help me. Holy God, where are you?

A very present help in trouble, my foot. Where are you? Have you
dropped me again? But I am not depressed, at least that. What is
wrong with me?

———

"Kathryn, can you hear me? Do you hear what I am saying?
I think you need to see a doctor. Did you call Dr. K. like I suggested? He's really a very nice guy, a very human doctor, the best
psychiatrist in the city. Nobody doesn't like Dr. K. Kathryn, do
you know why this is happening? Look, you need to be seen today.
I am calling Dr. K. right now."

———

"You are having a manic episode. I have some medicine that
will help. If you start the medicine now, you can prevent the cycle
from swinging out of control. I would suggest that we try you on
Depakote, which has been used for years to treat epilepsy, and
more recently to treat manic depression . . ."
Manic depression? Is that what you are saying I have? This is
ridiculous. Look, this is just a silly mistake. My therapist just
overreacted. She's very sweet but a bit overly protective . . . What
if I am just exaggerating, making this all up, and you are ready
to treat me like I am some epileptic convulsing on the floor . . .
I thank you very much for your concern. But I really don't want
to take any medicine . . . For how long? Two days? Five days? . . .
Six months? Maybe my *whole life?* Who is the crazy one here? . . .
This is absurd. You don't even know me. I have always been a little
nutty. This is normal for me . . . So let me get this straight, you
want me to continue the Zoloft to keep me from getting depressed,
and take the Depakote to keep me from getting too happy, and
take the Ativan to keep me from getting too panicky? You really
have a pill for every occasion, don't you? . . . Can I go now? No,
I know this is not a prison, but I didn't want to be rude. Yes, I
know we aren't really finished, but how are we supposed to reach
closure on this one? You want me to take drugs and I don't want

to . . . OK look, I really think you are blowing things out of pro-
portion, but go ahead and give me the prescription . . . No, don't
call it in, just give me the slip . . . I will talk to my husband about
it. He's the one who has to put up with me; he should have some
say in all of this.

> Almighty God, have mercy upon us, who, when troubled with the
> things that are past, lose faith, and life, and courage, and hope.
> So have mercy upon us, and uphold us, that we, being sustained
> by a true faith that Thou art merciful and forgiving, may go on
> in the life of the future to keep Thy commandments, to rejoice in
> Thy bounty, to trust in Thy mercy, and to hope in the eternal life.
> Grant unto all of us, whatsoever may betide us, to remember ever
> that it is all of Thy guidance, under Thy care, by Thy will; that
> so, in darkest days, beholding Thee we may have courage to go
> on, faith to endure, patience to bear, and hopefulness to hold out,
> even unto the end—Amen.
>
> George Dawson (1821–76)

I am damaged. Manic depressive. No one understands this, and
no one will understand this. Last night someone made a crack at
karate class that the brown belts doing their pinyans looked like
medication time at the state hospital. They were making a joke
at the expense of people not unlike me. There but for the grace of
God go I. No, even despite the grace of God go I. And, of course,
all of us, but those blokes with their sanity somewhat intact can
pretend that it has nothing to do with the grace of God, that fundamentally they are better than the sedated stooges at the state
hospital. Dear God, I thought you had humiliated me, chastened
me, taught me enough about my frailty and complete reliance
upon your sustaining grace. Have I not learned my lessons well
enough, that you must teach me yet again? Depression was bad
enough, but this is horrifying. To know that without these little
pills I might do something mortifying, embarrassing, dangerous.
I might actually try to fly. Maybe start directing traffic. People

simply cannot accept hypomania. Depressives are nonthreatening, but people are afraid of hypomaniacs.

<center>~~~~~</center>

"Mania is often followed by depression. A manic episode often will trigger a depressive episode. We have medicine to help."

<center>~~~~~</center>

Medicine. None of this is medicine. Medicine makes one better, cures a disease. These drugs only mask symptoms, and if the drug is removed, the symptom may still be there, or may not, and may return at some future unforeseen point. This is not medicine. These are just pills. Humiliating reminders that my brain has short-circuited.

I desperately do not want to take my medication. Depression is worse than awful, but hypomania, just under the edge of mania, is fun. Before it overflows into full-blown mania, it is remarkable. I am light, quick, brilliant, fascinating even to myself. I watch myself as though I were an actress on the stage. But being medicated for mania is painful at first, because I don't know the highs and have no excuse for the lows, and I feel dull and dead inside. The medication for mania takes away all the liveliness that I knew in hypomania. It makes my mouth dry, my bowels stop, my stomach ache. It puts on weight, which was a good thing at first, but later combined with an antidepressant it causes excessive weight gain. This can't be good for my health.

This is the point at which many people throw out the medication, or stop taking it to save it surreptitiously for the suicidal stages. I admit that throughout my depressions over the years that followed, I would garner stockpiles of ammunition like this against myself just in case I could not take the lows any longer. There would follow conversations with therapists and psychiatrists to convince me to dump the arsenal down the toilet. Stockpiling medication is probably one of the most dangerous habits a depressed person can fall into. Certainly I could have taken an overdose of ibuprofen for lack of anything else, but that would not have been as dangerous as an overdose of antidepressants or other psychiatric medication. If you know of anyone who has symptoms of mental illness, especially depression, make sure as possible that they are not stockpiling medication for future reference. All medicine that is not being taken at present should be thrown out. Convince them to give it to you, and flush it down the toilet. Don't put it in the garbage where it can be retrieved.

If you know someone who may be suicidal, do everything in your power to ensure that they have *no* access to weapons whatsoever. Remove from their homes all firearms, even if this means a squabble and a rupture in your relationship. A more severe and permanent rupture in the relationship could result. You may feel you are disrespecting the person's autonomy to override their wishes. But in the case of someone who may be suicidal, autonomy is exactly what can harm them.

In the end, there were two factors that kept me from deploying that arsenal, even though I did want to at certain points. I knew from the outside what it is like to survive the suicide of a loved one. I knew that my family would simply be devastated. As close as I may have come, I could not do that to them. I never wanted to hurt myself or anyone else. I just desperately wanted to end my own suffering. Even so, I never let my children's welfare out of my sight.

Other than my family, who I might say were a passive influence on me, since they were not aware at the time how much danger I was in, the active influence on me was my therapist, B. A petite woman, she has the emotional strength of a Sisyphus and used it to wrestle me out of the most dangerous times and to push me, ever up and inching down the hill again, finally back up to some degree of health. While I know that she would say it was my work, not hers, this is the way I see it.

During hypomania I felt completely different from the way I did at the depressive pole. Mania doesn't hurt the way depression does. Depression meant that every breath, every thought, every moment of consciousness hurt. Every particle of my consciousness ached, throbbed, stung. Mania was the opposite: every breath, every movement, every image before my eyes, every thought sparkled, glittered magically, filled me with ecstasy. Centrifugal motion, bliss.

At this point, thanks (ironically) to the medicine, I am not filled with ecstasy. Neither am I in agony. I just don't want to exist. I am tired—not physically, no, because the medicine is working. Heaven forbid I should be physically tired. Leave it to Western medicine to make a drug that provides productivity even during depressive episodes. But I am tired of existing inside of myself, don't want to be inside my own skin, am tired of feeling and talking and figuring out why I feel this way and that way, tired of putting off the inevitable, that I should return to the earth from which even I, another muddy Adam, was formed.

5

Darkness, Again

O Lord, help us not despise what we do not understand.

William Penn (1644–1718)

After hypomania comes the darkness, again. The doctor's medicine has managed to build a ceiling for the hypomania, to keep me from traveling too high. But there is as yet no floor for the depression. I am in the subbasement, bungeed from low to high to low again. With the darkness, I experience visions and voices. This is true of people with symptoms like mine from time to time. But the stigma of mental illness, evident in the jokes made by the healthy about the ill, is worse than the visions and voices. At least the visions and voices teach me something about myself and about God. The stigma teaches me nothing except about humanity's inhumanity to itself. Working despite the realities of this stigma, there are many who have suffered mental illness and yet were and are prodigious in their fields. This gives me hope: I want to be one of these prodigious ones as well, despite the reality and the stigma of mental illness.

Darkness, again. It comes and goes over the next several years. After five weeks on the Depakote, after I have swung from hypomania to depression again, the doctor wants me to try Lithium. Apparently that works well with one of the antidepressants I have not yet tried, Wellbutrin. But first I have to get on the Lithium, then get on the Wellbutrin, then come off the Zoloft that I have been on for four years. This whole process will take about a month. Sometime in that series of events I will come off the Depakote. Good. I can't stand it. Every time I forget to take the Depakote I start feeling normal again. Why am I taking this stuff?

I do hate these meds, yet I have to give them a try. For the sake of my family I must try to put up with this. Just try my best to stay out of the hospital. Do whatever I can to try to get better so as not to be hospitalized. I have a theory about these meds: the doctors give them to you to make you so sick that you resolve never again to complain about any of the symptoms! "Hey, doc, good to see you. I am feeling just fine. See you next week . . ." I sometimes have very little faith in their "medicines."

Darkness, again. This titrating of medicines will last for years, on and off, as my depressions flow from simply low to lower and back to simply low again. The trial of each medicine will take at least several weeks before we know whether it will work. One will last for a few months, leaving me only mildly depressed at best, and then it will "wear out." Then we will try another, and the side effects will be impossible to endure. Then we will try another, and the side effects will be impossible, but it is the only medication to make me significantly better. We layer medications throughout, trying to find the perfect cocktail for my brain. Through all this time, the hypomania is under control; depression is the plague.

> Discipline yourselves, keep alert. Like a roaring lion your adversary the devil prowls around, looking for someone to devour. Resist him, steadfast in your faith.
>
> 1 Peter 5:8–9a

Tell me about it. But if I were to say this to any of my doctors, I imagine they would think this was paranoia, or inappropriate religiosity, a symptom of my disease. Is it? I don't think so. Sometimes I do think that the roaring lion is in control of my disease, or maybe that my disease is wrought by the devil. My doctors would regard this as magical thinking—another symptom of disease. There are some things I simply cannot discuss with them. Religious experience is not something many of them are at all willing to take into account.

> There is therefore now no condemnation for those who are in Christ Jesus. For the law of the Spirit of life in Christ Jesus has set you free from the law of sin and of death.
>
> Romans 8:1–2

Help me, Lord, to remember this, to chew this cud, to digest it, to take it into my very heart, to carve it on to the very stone of my heart. Christ Jesus has set me free from the power of even these illnesses.

You really can't make jokes in a mental hospital. You have to be careful about what you say, because the doctors may take you seriously and think you are sicker than you really are. And you can't even mention that you have to be careful, or they will think you are paranoid. A sign of illness. Or am I just truly being paranoid?

> Abide with me; fast falls the eventide;
> The darkness deepens, Lord, with me abide;
> When other helpers fail, and comforts flee,
> Help of the helpless, Lord, abide with me. . . .
>
> I fear no foe, with thee at hand to bless;
> Ills have no weight, and tears no bitterness.

> Where is death's sting? Where grave, thy victory?
> I triumph still if thou abide with me.
>
> Henry F. Lyte (1793–1847)

Darkness, again. Today as I was driving home from my teaching job at a college up the shoreline, the highway started rolling up in smoke before my eyes. Pavement curling up like a burning page. *Abide with me.* The doctor says that during profound or prolonged depressions, this sort of thing can happen: I see things that aren't really there, I hear things that others don't hear. At seventy miles an hour, watching the road roll up like a scroll before me is, to say the least, startling. But the vision expressed the way I feel: the way ahead of me is disappearing, but I am hurtling nevertheless into the void. Of course I should not have been driving in this state. But even the mentally ill need to go where they need to go, just like the rest of the world.

> Peace I leave with you; my peace I give to you. I do not give to you
> as the world gives. Do not let your hearts be troubled, and do not
> let them be afraid.
>
> John 14:27

As I was planting some seeds, carefully poking them down into the soil and covering them lightly, I heard the verse "For you have died, and your life is hidden with Christ in God" (Col. 3:3). Like the seeds hidden snug under the soil, waiting for the power of nature to change them into sprouts, my life is hidden with Christ in the life of the triune God. I am not yet what I will become—thank God this is not "as good as it gets"! I am protected through the merciful layer of God's shielding of my life from all that would destroy it. And there is so much that seeks to tear my life away from God these days: the depression, the hypomania, the efforts to overcome the depression, and the desire to allow the hypomania's tornado in my mind and my soul. Despite all that I desire and all that I do not desire—both poles of the spectrum that would seem to exclude the Holy One—my life is hidden, protected, nurtured with Christ in God, in spite of myself. Such words of comfort. And to think I am taking medication to keep such voices at bay. God can work even despite the medication. And even through it.

Suffering is not eliminated by the resurrection but transformed by it. "I consider that the sufferings of this present time are not worth comparing with the glory about to be revealed to us. For the creation awaits with eager longing for the revealing of the children of God" (Rom. 8:18–19). The resurrection gives us hope for the future. "The creation itself will be set free from its bondage to decay. . . . For in hope we were saved. Now hope that is seen is not hope. For who hopes for what is seen? But if we hope for what we do not see, we wait for it with patience" (Rom. 8:21, 24–25). At the return of Jesus, death will be no more. His coming in glory will kill even the power of the last enemy, death. The promise to us is that, on that last day, God will wipe away every tear. But we still have tears in the present. Our bodies still die. In God's future, however, "death, thou shalt die" (John Donne, 1572–1631). The tree of life in that ancient garden becomes the cross that gives us life. This is the Christian hope: by the power of Jesus's resurrection, the first fruits of the general resurrection, we will be raised to joyous life with God.

The hope of the resurrection is not mere optimism, but leans the Christian life ever facing toward the future, not merely dwelling in the present. The Christian hope is not only for the individual Christian, nor only for the church itself. It is for all of creation, which was bound in decay by that first sin: "Cursed is the ground because of you; . . . thorns and thistles it shall bring forth for you" (Gen. 3:17–18). This curse of even the land and its increase will be retracted at the resurrection. All creation will be redeemed from pain and woe. Even for those with broken brains, this understanding of Christian hope can comfort and encourage. Sorrowing and sighing will be no more. Tears will be wiped away. Even refractory brains will be restored.

Save me, O God,
    for the waters have risen up to my neck.
I am sinking in deep mire,
    And there is no firm ground for my feet;
I have come into deep waters,
    and the torrent washes over me.
I have grown weary with my crying; my throat is inflamed.
    my eyes have failed from looking for my God.

                                              Psalm 69:1–3

Darkness, again. Prayer now is screaming, writhing, panting, hissing curses through clenched teeth. Who is this God who curses me and sends a cycle of curses?

Be angry but do not sin; do not let the sun go down on your anger.

                                              Ephesians 4:26

Angry, yes, that is my life's song these days. To know that Scripture recognizes that we get angry, and allows the expression of anger, is a great comfort. And how psychologically healing that Scripture tells us to express anger but not to let it spend the night with us.

Where can I go from your spirit?
    Where can I flee from your presence?
If I climb up to heaven, you are there;
    if I make the grave my bed, you are there also.
If I take the wings of the morning
    and dwell in the uttermost parts of the sea,
even there your hand will lead me,
    and your right hand hold me fast.
If I say, "Surely the darkness will cover me,
    and the light around me turn to night,"
darkness is not dark to you;
the night is as bright as the day,
    for darkness and light to you are both alike.
                                              Psalm 139:6–11

Even if I don't see you, don't want to see you, feel you have abandoned me, want to abandon you, even there you are with me. This
I can feel only after coming out of Sheol. But I look back and
know you were there. Darkness is not dark to you. Even though
I may feel that darkness is my only companion, to know that the
darkness and the light are alike to you is great comfort.

Spring should come soon.

While the mentally ill cannot make jokes around their doctors,
plenty of people make jokes about those who live with mental illnesses. The reality may be funny to others, but to those who are
mentally ill, not much of this is funny at all. An advertisement I
saw on a billboard in a train station showed a rock climber dan-
gling from a rope, with the text "What's this maniac doing? He
forgot his sunscreen." This was by the American Association of
Dermatologists. Valentine's Day of 2005 brought the "Crazy for
U" teddy bear wearing a straitjacket. The National Association
of the Mentally Ill registered a public complaint. The 1927 silent
film *Jeanne d'Arc* has a scene in which it is said that this movie was
"discovered" in the closet of a mental institution. While watching
this, a whole crowd laughed, except for me, of course. I reckon
that people think mental patients are off their rockers, completely
detached, unbalanced, even scary. While that may be the case for
some of us at times, it is not necessarily so. People with mental
illnesses are suffering; they are not funnier than anyone else. I
think others laugh and are threatened by us out of nervousness
and discomfort. After all, sanity is a thin veneer on most folk. The
difference between the "normal" and "ill" is that ill folk have to
admit that they are broken. Jokes only promote the stigma. Stop
joking.

The worst thing about mental illness, besides the pain, is this
very stigma. The pointing. The staring. The laughing. Stigma
draws its energy from fear of the unknown, fear of the other
who is not like us. Stigma creates fear both of and in those of us
who live with mental illnesses. It directs the fear of those who are
healthy towards those who are ill.

I was so ill that at times I couldn't move. Yet because of the stigma, I didn't want to tell my boss why I couldn't come in to work. I had supervisors and colleagues whom I never told. I realize now that I should have been honest and told them just as I would have if I had had a fever, but at the time I didn't trust them with the news that I had a mental illness—one that would never leave me. How could I go back to work after revealing that news?

Indeed, writing this book is risky business. Stigma against people who live with mental illness can be so strong. How will people trust my intellectual and spiritual capacities if I once had difficulties with my memory, personality, and even speech and muscle control? If I actually thought the unthinkable, to take my own life? I am a priest, a writer, a theologian. How could I ever go back to my work? How would I be trusted by my rector, by my parish, by my bishop, by my colleagues in the academy? One friend, a professor of theology, actually said about another friend who had been through electroconvulsive therapy, "His career is finished." Obviously I never told her about my own problems. And so although I was hospitalized five times, most of my employers did not know. My bishop knew that I was ill, and was very understanding. A priest cannot keep this kind of news from her bishop. Most people just seemed to think I was oddly unreliable, or reliably odd.

One thing to recognize about mental illness is that it does not necessarily mean the sufferer has a character flaw. It may mean this, but it may not. The one who lives with mental illness may be the kind of person you might actually want for a friend, not an insidious, manipulative, lying cheat or a mass murderer. Part of the tragedy of stigma is that people do not understand that those who live with mental illness can be quite normal in many ways.

Prominent people throughout history exhibited symptoms of mental illness but during their stable times were able to be prolific artists. I think of William Cowper (1731–1800), poet and hymn writer who wrote such chestnuts as "O for a Closer Walk with Thee," "Jesus, Where'er Thy People Meet," "God Moves in a Mysterious Way," and many others. At more than one point Cowper attempted taking his own life. He was committed to a psychiatric hospital for a time. Author of the famous hymn "Amazing Grace," John Newton was Cowper's pastor and collaborator on some of his hymns. Apparently Newton saved Cowper from suicide on more than one occasion. Because of his mental illness, Cowper was not able to hold down a steady job, yet he wrote profound hymns and poetry. Even those who scorned evangelical "Methodists" read Cowper's poems and sang his hymns. And still do. He and Newton both addressed and sought to overturn many social ills of their day, among them the African slave trade.

> God moves in a mysterious way,
> His wonders to perform;
> He plants his footsteps in the sea
> And rides upon the storm.
>
> Ye fearful saints, fresh courage take;
> The clouds ye so much dread
> Are big with mercy, and shall break
> In blessings on your head.
>
> Judge not the Lord by feeble sense,
> But trust him for his grace;
> Behind a frowning providence
> He hides a smiling face.
>
> Blind unbelief is sure to err
> And scan his work in vain;
> God is his own interpreter,
> And he will make it plain.

The sense that God's storm clouds are great even with mercy, that his frowning providence hides a smiling face, that God is the interpreter of his own work are themes that give comfort to my depressed mind. Mercy is hidden in the storm; God's smiling face hides behind the frown of providence. So even the hiddenness of God can be a comfort.

Christina Rossetti (1830–94), also a hymnwriter and poet, suffered from mental and physical illnesses throughout her life. Yet she did not let this slow her down. During her healthier times, and even while she was sick, she was actively writing. She authored, among many other works, the Christmas carol "In the Bleak Midwinter."

> In the bleak midwinter, frosty wind made moan,
> Earth stood hard as iron, water like a stone;
> Snow had fallen, snow on snow, snow on snow,
> In the bleak midwinter long ago.
>
> Our God, heaven cannot hold him, nor earth sustain;
> Heaven and earth shall flee away, when he comes to reign;
> In the bleak midwinter, a stable place sufficed
> The Lord God almighty, Jesus Christ.
>
> Angels and archangels may have gathered there,
> Cherubim and seraphim throngéd the air;
> But his mother only, in her maiden bliss,
> Worshiped the beloved with a kiss.
>
> What can I give him, poor as I am?
> If I were a shepherd, I would bring a lamb;
> If I were a wise man, I would do my part;
> Yet what I can I give him—Give him my heart.

Again comes through the paradox of the hiddenness of God even in the incarnation, the high point of the very presence of God. Neither heaven nor earth can hold God, and yet a stable will suffice to shelter the Babe of Bethlehem.

Rossetti, writing under the nom de plume Ellen Alleyn, was hailed by the public as a literary success. Her first public poems appeared in the *Athenaeum* when she was only eighteen. Her writings reflect her deep religious devotion. She was a high church Anglican and enthusiast of Tractarianism, a conservative catholic movement within the Anglican Church. As a girl, Rossetti was passionate, vivacious, and quick-tempered yet even to the point of self-harm. She apparently once cut herself with scissors after being punished for a minor offense. As an adolescent, she contracted an unexplained illness with physical and mental symptoms. Her religiosity was called into question as cause or symptom of her illness. After she returned to health, Rossetti became even more intensely devoted to her religious observance. The questions I have are these: Why was her religiosity impugned as being inappropriately severe? How does one determine such a thing, and who is to determine it in our day: psychiatrists or priests? Are psychiatrists qualified to make such a judgment?

> The strong are not always vigorous, the wise not always ready, the brave not always courageous, and the joyous not always happy.
>
> Charles Haddon Spurgeon (1834–92)

Another preacher who seems to have suffered from symptoms of mental illness is Charles H. Spurgeon, the great nineteenth-century London preacher. He fought depression and severe anxiety throughout his lifetime. Yet he persisted in preaching throughout his mental and physical illnesses. Over the course of his fifty-eight years, he delivered some 3,500 sermons. He also authored 135 books. This was all from a man who declared that he hated writing.

"Depression comes over me whenever the Lord is preparing a larger blessing for my ministry. It has now become to me a prophet in rough clothing. A John the Baptist, heralding the nearer coming of my Lord's richer benison." Clearly Spurgeon felt about his depression much as I do about mine. Out of it comes a blessing, even though while in it not much but agony can be perceived. In this sense, God sends suffering in order to teach. "If the Christian did not sometimes suffer heaviness he would begin to grow too proud, and think too much of himself." This comment is open to criticism from secular therapists, who tend to understand depressives as having a poor self-image. "But you must think more highly of yourself, protect yourself more, be less concerned for your flock

to your own detriment, Spurgeon," they might say. That is clearly
not the way he saw the situation.

Word has it that the Niebuhr brothers, Reinhold (1892–1971)
and H. Richard (1894–1962), also suffered symptoms of depression. They were respectively considered the finest American ethicist
and theologian of their day. Reinhold taught at Union Seminary in
New York, and his younger brother taught at Yale Divinity School
in Connecticut. Among H. Richard's noted works are *Christ and
Culture*, *The Meaning of Revelation*, and *The Kingdom of God
in America*. H. Richard apparently spent time in the Yale Psychiatric Institute, the predecessor of the hospital in which I spent
time decades after him. More widely known among Americans,
his older brother Reinhold wrote *The Children of Light and the
Children of Darkness*, *The Interpretation of Christian Ethics*,
and *The Nature and Destiny of Man*, among other works. He
is likely the (usually uncredited) author of the famous Serenity
Prayer now used by Alcoholics Anonymous the world over. He is
also credited with being the author of the famous triad which has
been so helpful to me personally:

> Nothing that is worth doing can be achieved in a lifetime; therefore
> we must be saved by hope.

> Nothing we do, however virtuous, can be accomplished alone;
> therefore we are saved by love.

> Nothing which is true or beautiful or good makes complete sense
> in any immediate context of history; therefore we must be saved
> by faith.

In fact, a long train of famous artists have struggled against the
ravages of mental illness. According to Kay Redfield Jamison in her
Touched with Fire, a crew of prolific artists shared more in common than simply talent. They also apparently shared the suffering
from symptoms of mental illnesses. Among them were Charles
Baudelaire (1821–67), Samuel Taylor Coleridge (1772–1834), his

son Hartley Coleridge (1796–1849), Emily Dickinson (1830–86), Gerard Manley Hopkins (1844–89), Victor Hugo (1802–85), John Bunyan (1628–88), Charles Dickens (1812–70), Ralph Waldo Emerson (1803–82), Graham Greene (1904–91), Mary Shelley (1797–1851), and George Frederick Handel (1685–1759). In many of these cases the illnesses were complicated by self-medication with alcohol and opium in a day when no other medication was available. Just a few contemporary examples of highly talented celebrities who have lived with mental illnesses are Art Buchwald, Rosemary Clooney, Dick Cavett, Patty Duke, Jane Pauley, Kay Redfield Jamison, Elyn Saks, William Stegner, and Mike Wallace.

Many other famous people who could not bear their symptoms took their own lives: Sylvia Plath (1932–63), Anne Sexton (1928–74), Ernest Hemingway (1899–1961), Virginia Wolff (1882–1941), and Vincent van Gogh (1853–90), just to name a few. Each of these individuals contributed to our culture and society despite their illnesses.

I wonder how many of them, had they lived, would have blessed us with even more prose, poetry, music, and art. We simply don't know how much our society is being robbed today of creative talent by these illnesses. Mental illnesses, especially if they are treated promptly and effectively, are not a death sentence on one's contributions to society. And the fact that some people have risen above the stigma of mental illness to lead productive lives gives me hope for my own work.

Christian hope means that time is important. The Christian life is not just a circular spinning into nothingness but drives toward the goal at the end of time, the healing of all creation by the love of God. Time bears its purpose out in bringing us ever closer to the will of God in the redemption of creation. But in my darkness, yet again, I have learned something about time and mental illness. This kind of illness is hell, just unrelenting hell. That is because in depression time stands still. The essence of being depressed is the stillness, the molasses-in-January thickness of time. It is like the converse of the saying "Time flies when you're having fun."

Time does fly during hypomanic streaks, but my depressive black holes are just the darkness and void of nothingness, where not even time moves. Time does not march on for the miserably depressed. If time moved, maybe I could get somewhere, get out even if only inch by agonizing inch, out of this muck. In the midst of this sluggish hanging of time, all I can do is hold on and ask God to abide with me in the void. If only time would even crawl rather than slither, I would be in less agony. *Abide with me.*

I try to remember that it is the creeping slowness of time that allows the crocus to push its way through the frozen earth. If the crocus moved any faster, it would destroy itself in its struggle against the ice. And the slow but sure movement of the crocus is a sign of the end of the winter. Maybe the slowness of time, then, is God's mercy. I just have to remember that.

> The peace of God, it is no peace,
> But strife closed in the sod.
> Yet, Christians, pray for but one thing:
> That marv'lous peace of God.
>   William Alexander Percy
>   (1885–1942)

God's strange gift of time. Depression can be seen as a form of intensely painful boredom. The future fails to draw us forward; the past terrifies, haunts; the present hangs heavy. There is no melancholy for the passing of time. There is only furtive wishing it away. To be rid of it, to be drowned in its billows instead of carried aloft. There is no eager expectation of the next wave of happiness. Time for the mentally ill brain is stuck. It is not a gift but a curse. Yet at the very beginning of time, even before God creates the sun and stars to mark time, God creates "evening and morning, the first day." Time is in fact a gift of God to create the space for our living of our days before the Creator. Depression subverts this knowledge.

Time for the mentally ill brain even folds in on itself, plays back and forth on itself, drops off the cliff of present experience.

Sometimes I can in a flash go into a deep depression, as though the lights in the room were suddenly turned off. Some eight years after my postpartum depression began, we were on vacation in Guadeloupe. We left our darkened, cool room, and the moment I stepped outside into the light of day, I was stricken with a profound depression. The exotic birds, the gorgeous flowers and plantings, the blue sky, the sandy beach, the very fact that we were on vacation suddenly made me sick to my core. The birds were miserable, the flowers stank with rottenness, the blue sky washed gray, the white sands dimmed green, and the idea of the relaxation of vacation distressed me unbearably. Everything struck me as painful. Unfortunately this did not turn off as quickly as it turned on, and I was left in yet another depression for many long months following. Even after the electroconvulsive therapy, after rounds and rounds of medication and hundreds of hours of "talk" therapy, I kept falling into the darkness, again.

Come, Lord Jesus, you for whom darkness is as light, remove this veil from my face and enable me to see you.

> Come my Way, my Truth, my Life,
> Such a Way as gives us breath,
> Such a Truth as ends all strife,
> Such a Life as killeth death.
> George Herbert (1593–1633)

6

Hospital

Lord Jesus Christ, you are for me medicine when I
    am sick;
you are my strength when I need help;
you are life itself when I fear death;
you are the way when I long for heaven;
you are light when all is dark;
you are my food when I need nourishment.

Ambrose of Milan (340–97)

I had been taking many different medications in a series, trying
to find the ones that would "work." This was five years after my
postpartum depression, which never really left me consistently.
Only many years after that, with the combination of the last four
medications, have I felt truly better. I have tried the many meds in
differing constellations and combinations: Prozac, Paxil, Atavan,
Luvox, Zoloft, Celexa, Wellbutrin, Serzone, Effexor, Buspar, Depakote, Topamax, Zyprexa, Geodon, Parnate, Ambien, Lamictal,
Abilify, and Nardil, with Lithium almost throughout. At times the

medication felt less like weapons against my symptoms and more like Saul's heavy armor on the young David. They made me shake, quiver, oversleep. They left me confused, disoriented, amnesiac, unable to pronounce even my own name. I would fall asleep anywhere, including at the wheel when driving or when standing at prayer. The confusion has been one of the worst problems for me. I once had such a clear mind. The side effects were so unbearable at times that as David chose to take off his armor, I once or twice chose to come off my medication. I got immediately worse. The armor went back on. I have learned not to come off medication.

One class of these medications in particular can be dangerous: the MAOIs (Monoamine Oxidase Inhibitors) such as Nardil and Parnate. They require a strict diet, entirely cutting out cheese, chocolate, red wine, caffeine, smoked meats, and soy sauce, to mention just some of the foods. I have on more than one occasion ended up in the hospital emergency room with blood pressure alarmingly high from a reaction to a dangerous food. There was risk of stroke and/or heart attack. MAOIs were at one point critically useful to me but later almost killed me. I can never take them again.

The other day I read a text from the Babylonian Talmud (completed sixth century AD) that said the cure for depression is to eat red meat broiled over coals and to drink diluted wine. This sounds no less strange than the prescription of antidepressants, the specific function of which the medical world really does not have any greater knowledge of than did the Talmud of the effects of meat and red wine.

During my depression after Guadeloupe, I became increasingly sick while trying medication after medication that had no effect. I was in so much psychic pain that I could not bear it. My therapist suggested the hospital; I immediately rejected the idea. A psychiatric hospital? Maybe for other people, for the weak, but not for me. I was embarrassed and ashamed just at the mention of the idea. My first therapist had brought it up as a possibility that might be helpful when I had postpartum depression after our daughter was born. This was some five years later, but I was still adamant about not going to the hospital. However, over months of agony, my defenses against the hospital broke down, and I finally agreed to enter what was then called Yale Psychiatric Institute (now Yale Psychiatric Hospital) for a then-undetermined amount of time. The stay ended up being short, just about a week.

> Out of the depths I cry unto thee, O LORD!
>   Lord, hear my voice!
> Let thy ears be attentive
>   to the voice of my supplications!
>
> If thou, O LORD, shouldst mark iniquities,
>   Lord, who could stand?
> But there is forgiveness with thee,
>   that thou mayest be feared.
>
> I wait for the LORD, my soul waits,
>   and in his word I hope;
> my soul waits for the LORD
>   more than watchmen for the morning,
>   more than watchmen for the morning.
>
> O Israel, hope in the LORD!
>   For with the LORD there is steadfast love,
>   and with him is plenteous redemption.
> And he will redeem Israel
>   from all his iniquities.
>
> Psalm 130 RSV

Waiting on the LORD when one is mentally ill takes extreme effort. Yet the soul does wait for the LORD more than watchmen for the morning, with that dead-tired heavy expectation of the sun's expected rise. Yes, even though I was not sure that the sun would really rise, that the LORD would really come. It was only through reading the Bible and the prayers of others, in particular the Psalms, that I came to be able to wait, to hope in God's plenteous redemption. Or at least to acknowledge that some had that hope and that I wanted to be in the community that had that hope, even if I could not feel it.

> O LORD, my heart is not lifted up,
>   my eyes are not raised too high;
> I do not occupy myself with
>   things too great and too marvelous for me.
> But I have calmed and quieted my soul,
>   like a child quieted at its mother's breast;
>   like a child that is quieted is my soul.
>
> O Israel, hope in the LORD
>   from this time forth and for evermore.
>   Psalm 131 RSV

Like a child quieted at its mother's breast. I love that image. I remember when my son, our first child, was an infant, he would get so hungry and grumpy, but within seconds of his latching on to the breast, the grimace would leave his face and a flood of delight would spread over him. A child satisfied at its mother's breast. Dear God, give me your milk and quiet my soul; give me the peace of feeding on you.

Teaching. At college, in the classroom. What in God's name am I doing here, up in front of all these young people? What if I melt down here in front of them? I am supposed to be going to the hospital later today, and here I am leading a discussion for some ninety college students.

My therapist, B., called to say that I had two options: either the geriatric ward at Yale–New Haven Hospital (the "medical" hospital) or the adolescent ward at Yale Psychiatric Institute (YPI). I said that we should just forget the whole hospitalization thing. Just forget it. She didn't agree to that plan. During the day, a spot opened for me on the adult unit at YPI.

Again, my mother was visiting to help out at the time. Told her that B. wanted me in the hospital. As calmly as if I were saying that I was going to the store for milk. Inside I was a mess. Mom had no idea this was a real possibility, because I had successfully been convincing her I was well. Mom gave a pained yelp, asking if it had really gotten that bad. Yes, I replied, turning and quickly walking away. Can't stand the pain I cause others; the pain I cause myself is too much in and of itself. Packed my suitcase. Had set out most of what I would need the previous night, so this was quick. Asked Mom to drive me. Didn't want her with me when I checked in. Couldn't bear to see her face, hear the worry in her voice.

The good thing about being in the hospital: you can block out the world. You don't have to respond to people if you can't, and they won't take offense. If you can't handle your family's worry, you can just cut it off, just like all the external stresses: lift the needle off the record. Push the pause button on the CD. That is what the hospital was for me.

> I loathe my life;
>> I will give free utterance to my complaint;
>> I will speak in the bitterness of my soul.
>>> Job 10:1

Yes, Job, I understand how you could loathe life. Certainly I understand. But how can I loathe the life given me by a good Creator? This has got to have an element of evil. Clearly an element of sickness, of illogic, of twisted thinking. Yet I do not actively participate in this. I try to participate actively in prayer, in the exercise of faith, hope, and love. I pray daily, and this helps immensely. But it is all removed from me, as though through a soundproof wall, through bulletproof glass. I am alone. Darkness is my closest companion.

> Bring us, O Lord God, at our last awakening into the house and gate
> of heaven, to enter into that gate and dwell in that house, where

there shall be no darkness nor dazzling, but one equal light; no noise nor silence, but one equal music; no fears nor hopes, but one equal possession; no ends nor beginnings, but one equal eternity; in the habitations of your glory and dominion, world without end.

John Donne (1572–1631)

There is light. Would that I could go there now. But it is more worthy to stay here for your benefit, my husband, my children. How could I do this to you—rush God's grace, usurp it, and reach into the heavenly places, only to choose in reality the darkness? How could I do that to them? They would simply never recover. I must not, I must not, I cannot, but I want desperately to be removed from this pain. I don't want to kill myself, just to be relieved of this darkness, emptiness, lack of care. Sleep. Sleep is one way out. Sleep just for a while, to face it all over again upon waking.

My husband, Matthew, just wants to help. He keeps asking me what he can do. He says that he feels so helpless. He is indeed helpless, and so am I. There is nothing he can do. Yet maybe there is. I tell him not to treat me like an invalid. When I can't get up, when I can't crack a smile through my plaster mask of a face, when I can't do anything but weep, just hold my hand. *But please don't be in pain for me.* Because then I can see that on your face, and it makes my pain worse. Just treat me in a matter-of-fact way: Kathryn is depressed again. Or when I am hypomanic, don't get scared of me. Don't get mad at me just because I talk too much, have too much energy, burst at the seams with ideas for the garden, the house, vacations, books. It is not my fault that I swing from one extreme to the other. I know loving me right now is a big challenge. But that's how I can be helped.

> How firm a foundation, ye saints of the Lord,
> is laid for your faith in God's excellent Word!
> What more can he say than to you he has said,
> to you that for refuge to Jesus have fled?

"Fear not, I am with thee; O be not dismayed!
For I am thy God and will still give thee aid;
I'll strengthen thee, help thee and cause thee to stand,
Upheld by my righteous, omnipotent hand.

"When through the deep waters I call thee to go,
the rivers of woe shall not thee overflow;
for I will be with thee, thy troubles to bless,
And sanctify to thee thy deepest distress.

"When through fiery trials thy pathway shall lie,
My grace, all sufficient, shall be thy supply;
the flame shall not hurt thee; I only design
thy dross to consume, and thy gold to refine.

"The soul that to Jesus hath fled for repose,
I will not, I will not desert to its foes;
that soul, though all hell should endeavor to shake,
I'll never, no never, no never forsake."
                                         John Rippon (1751–1836)

This hymn would always make me cry when I was depressed. I always wondered, what did my parish think as I wept during many of the hymns? But no one ever asked. Maybe they never noticed? Or maybe they were too embarrassed for my sake to say anything, too polite. "That soul, though all hell should endeavor to shake, I'll never, no never, no never forsake." I felt entirely forsaken, but God's promise in Christ to me was overwhelmingly comforting.

Walked into YPI on my own, suitcase in hand. Apparently they are not used to seeing this. The security guards at the entrance thought I must be lost. "This is a hospital," they said, as though I didn't look like a potential patient. Emergency room shuntees, or those forcibly admitted by family or friends, but someone alone? A relatively attractive, sane-looking woman (for all intents and purposes in their evidently dulled imaginations) couldn't belong here. They were amused. I was not. This is not funny.

After this Job opened his mouth and cursed the day of his
birth. Job said:

> Let the day perish in which I was born,
>   and the night that said,
>   "A man-child is conceived."
> Let that day be darkness!
>   May God above not seek it,
>   or light shine on it.
> Let gloom and deep darkness claim it.
>   Let clouds settle upon it;
>   let the blackness of the day terrify it.
> That night—let thick darkness seize it!
>   let it not rejoice among the days of the year;
>   let it not come into the number of the months.
> Yes, let that night be barren;
>   let no joyful cry be heard in it. . . .
> For my sighing comes like my bread,
>   and my groanings are poured out like water.
> Truly the thing that I fear comes upon me,
>   and what I dread befalls me.
> I am not at ease, nor am I quiet;
>   I have no rest; but trouble comes.
>
> Job 3:3–7, 24–26

Bags checked before I could enter the locked ward—somewhat
like at the airport, but even more stringently than after 9/11. They
were scoured for any item with which I might harm myself. They
removed from my belongings my mirrored compact, my pencil
sharpener. Implication: I might use these to harm myself. Why
then didn't they confiscate my belt, my shoelaces? They frisked me,
made me disrobe just to make sure I was not concealing something.
What? A razor blade? A hedge trimmer? Lawn mower, maybe,
tucked neatly into my bra? For sure. They didn't make me remove
my brain. That's the only thing that could harm me now.

Interviews with nurses, doctors. Some of the patients do make this place look like a nuthouse, to use an unfortunate term. I am among the most "normal" looking of them, whatever "normal" might mean here. Funny that I should look normal. But I suppose I do. I am still thin, soon however to gain weight in the pattern of most patients who are on heavy psychiatric medication. I dress in jeans that fit, without the derriere hanging out or the stomach peeking through. I put my hair up in a clip because it is dirty: depression makes taking a shower feel like climbing Mount Everest. Many patients stay in their pajamas all day. I will come to that too after a few days. My face and arms are clear of the cigarette burns and self-inflicted wounds on other patients. I speak my "educated talk," while most of the patients are less schooled than I am. *Why is this?* I wonder. My religious life also separates me from the others, who for the most part think my concern with prayer must be a psychological glitch. I seem to be taken for "normal," like one of the staff. One of the other patients actually asked, "Do you work here? You don't look like a patient." I felt like yelling: but just look inside my mind. Then you would see that I am a patient.

Ate dinner on the ward. Tuna sandwich. Not yet allowed off the unit. Patients are on fifteen-minute checks. Every dashed fifteen minutes they check on us throughout the night to make sure we are still alive and not trying to harm ourselves. This is so terribly humiliating, but I know I have to go through with it. For the sake of my family. For me? Can't get there right now. The first time I got checked at night, I startled and sat straight up in bed. "Oh nothing, just checks," said the nurse. I learned to sleep through them as time went by, and eventually got used to them.

In the Yale Psychiatric Institute, they usually do not put patients in restraints, except maybe in the most severe cases of agitation. I never saw this happen, although I have seen patients be taken into the isolation room. They do not treat patients as Hollywood portrays it. That is because most people there are not in the condition that would call for such treatment. Besides, we now have medication that can substitute for restraints to sedate the patient instead of tying us down. I have never had to endure any of this. But I am sure that it would be completely embarrassing and enraging to be put in restraints.

YPI is somewhat like a hotel, just a hotel that you can't leave anytime you want. One visitor said with surprise that the unit seemed more like a college dorm than a hospital. It is indeed like a hospital, but one in which you have security but no privacy. The units are locked. At mealtimes they take us downstairs, provided we have "privileges," a euphemism for the assessment that we won't try to escape or get violent. One worker leads fifteen or so patients, and one follows. They count the group at the top of the stairs and count again at the bottom. The cafeteria is unlocked for our entry, and locked again behind us. The food is not as horrible as I had been expecting.

The unit I was on had some eight or ten bedrooms, mostly doubles, with two quads. There was a room with a piano and large table where activities took place. A pay telephone was our only link to the outside world. But because our money had been confiscated, the hall phone served only to receive calls. Cell phones were not allowed. There were three bathrooms on the floor for the patients, and laundry machines. There was a small kitchen area that opened on to a common room. Weighing in was the first routine of the day for those of us who were underweight. There was a living room at the far end of the unit where we shared our daily personal goals. At the beginning of the day each patient set a goal for herself and then at the end of the day evaluated how she had or had not reached it. This was sometimes the only one of the groups that bordered on therapy that I was well enough to participate in.

My goal was always to say the Daily Office, something that took at most only twenty-five minutes twice a day in the "real world." In the hospital and in my ill brain it took most of the day. This lent new meaning to the phrase "*Daily* Office." Reading the Psalms, collects, Scripture, and prayers was nearly impossible. Concentration was no longer a faculty I possessed. Each word seemed to swim in front of my eyes. But I was determined that this should be part of my therapy, even if my doctors seemed a little concerned about my "religiosity." Overly religious speech and ideas can be considered a symptom of illness.

Sometimes, very occasionally, there was art therapy. I remember once making a clay vase and being so calmed by the silky texture of the clay. I was surprised that I could actually make something that pleased me. There were staff-led games to keep the less ill among us from sheer boredom. There were on rare occasions other therapy groups, and an exercise class.

I was under the impression that the chaplain visited two days a week. She was a warm and compassionate woman whom I had known previously from our mutual church affiliations. Upon seeing me, she exclaimed, "And what are you doing here?" Not the best way to greet someone who already feels ashamed about being in the hospital. Part of her job was leading the Spirituality Group, which I attended only once. It was generically religious. I am not generically religious. Another of the chaplain's tasks was to conduct spiritual intake assessments. This entailed in part filling out forms on each patient. Home address? What religion? What church/ synagogue? Name of religious leader? When she asked if there was anything she could do for me, I asked her to pray with me. She did, quite willingly, but then never offered again.

<hr />

Laughing Christina. She hears voices almost constantly and laughs, even at the most inappropriate times. Might be nice to hear such amusements. Better than hearing voices that make you weep or scream. Then there is Sophie, the old woman in the wheelchair who is convinced that the staff is getting ready to kill her and pleads quietly with me to tell her what they are planning. Douglas, who at group meetings spells his name letter by letter when called on, D-O-U-G-L-A-S, and lets out a belly laugh, gleeful. He does not say much else. Steven, who is so depressed that his vocal cords simply do not function. Daniel, whose wife left him because she just could not bear his depression. The others fade into forgetfulness.

They let us out of the building after meals into the courtyard, the unbreachable fortress walls surrounding us and keeping us "safe." Fresh Air Run, they call it. Instead of running, the patients would stand around and smoke. Stale Air Slouch.

At one point when I was hospitalized, maybe the first or second time, they actually took us on occasion to a gym with exercise bikes. I always went when the opportunity arose. The bikes were old and useless, but even the short walk to the gym was a relief of sorts.

Almighty God, whose most dear Son went not up to joy but first he suffered pain, and entered not into glory before he was cruci-fied: mercifully grant that we, walking in the way of the cross, may find it none other than the way of life and peace; through Jesus Christ our Lord.

Collect for Friday, BCP, 99

Today is Friday, March 13. One of my childhood friends was killed by a falling tree on Thursday the twelfth. Ever since then, I am not afraid of Friday the thirteenth. Superstition is, of course, an-tithetical to the Christian faith. But I don't even need that to push it away. Tragedy strikes even on the days when you don't expect it. Why scout it out by setting apart certain days to fear?

Be my strong rock, a castle to keep me safe;
you are my crag and my stronghold.
Psalm 71:3

This hospital is God's castle to keep me safe. A place where I can-not hurt myself, where I am protected from my own brain, where God has tucked me away from the stresses of my life. I can sleep. I can zone. I can completely avoid talking to anyone, except of course the doctors and social workers. I don't have to pretend here. Christ is my castle to keep me safe. He has entered the hell of this place for me, has gone before me, and stays with me.

An alternative therapy to medication and "talk therapy" that is administered at the hospital is electroconvulsive therapy (ECT). While antidepressants are effective about 50 percent of the time, ECT (sometimes called "shock therapy" by those who do not understand it) is apparently effective 75–90 percent of the time. It is prescribed for those suffering various sorts of mental illnesses, but mostly depressions. ECT consists of administering a small amount of electricity to the head, which induces a seizure of the brain alone. This lasts only a few seconds. At YPI, treatments are generally given three times per week for a few weeks or more.

While it can be terrifying the first few times because it is unfamiliar, it is not the horrendous torture portrayed by Hollywood in which the patient thrashes and screams in agony. This may have been the way ECT was once administered, but now it is much more humane. Even still, patients for whom ECT treatments have been recommended tend to be exceedingly wary. I have known people who were terribly depressed and who still pushed away ECT as an option because they were afraid of what it might do to their brain. But the alternatives are not very pleasant either, considering what the mental illness is doing to the brain.

Even though ECT is stigma-loaded and can affect short-term memory, it is usually a quite valuable treatment. Don't watch *One Flew Over the Cuckoo's Nest* or *A Beautiful Mind* before taking ECT. In the latter movie, one of the patient's seizures was induced not by electricity but by insulin injection. This is potentially deadly and has been outmoded for decades. The Hollywood nightmares may sell tickets at the box office, but they really do not reflect the actual experience of the patient in ECT.

During present-day ECT treatments the patient is given general anesthesia, so is unaware of what is happening. In my experience, having a tooth filled is far more traumatic. In an ECT treatment, there is no crying out in pain or thrashing in fear. In fact, I have been told that there are no bodily convulsions at all. A muscle relaxant is administered along with the anesthesia. Bodily movements may sometimes include the wiggling of a toe, the flickering of an eyelid, or the contracting of the jaw muscles. But the convulsion is restricted to the brain itself.

The procedure is as follows at YPI. I am not permitted to eat or drink after midnight the night before until after the treatment. This is standard protocol when general anesthesia is administered in any medical procedure. In the morning the attendant brings me down to the treatment room. I climb up onto a gurney on which they will prep me and wheel me into the procedure room.

> God is our refuge and strength,
>   a very present help in trouble.
> Therefore we will not fear, though the earth be moved,
>   and though the mountains be toppled into the depths
>   of the sea;
> Though its waters rage and foam,
>   and though the mountains tremble at its tumult.
> The LORD of hosts is with us;
>   the God of Jacob is our stronghold.
>
>   Psalm 46:1–4

They fit me with a blood pressure cuff that will stay on my arm to monitor my blood pressure throughout the treatment. They ask me some basic questions to gauge the state of my cognition: What is your name? What day is it? Where are you? They take my temperature and ask me to rate my mood on a scale from one to ten. They attach electrodes to my torso to monitor my heart rate throughout the treatment. A nurse inserts an intravenous line into my arm. She prepares what I assume are the electrodes for the treatment: round metal plates about one and a half inches in diameter with holes in the center. She spreads on them a clear gel with the consistency and appearance of KY Jelly. Then she secures the electrodes to my head with a white band. Grommets secure the metal plates to the white band. I must look like a wounded soldier with my head wrapped in a gauze bandage. They wheel me into the procedure room, and when they are ready, they insert into the IV the anesthesia and muscle relaxant. For a millisecond I can feel the anesthesia burn as it travels from my IV up past the underside of my arm and past the back of my throat. I can sense the anesthesia in my mouth and nose, a rubbing alcohol or nail polish odor and taste. Then nothing.

After what seems like a moment but is probably a few minutes I wake up to the nurse calling me out of my rubbing alcohol/nail polish stupor. I am nauseated from the anesthesia. Slowly I am able to sit up and am walked back to the locked unit. I zigzag to my room and sleep off the anesthesia for a few hours. After that I have a headache. Surprise, surprise. I have just had my head zapped with electricity. For subsequent treatments, they add an antinausea medication and a strong anti-inflammatory to my IV before the procedure, and the negative aftereffects are no longer bothersome.

> Bless the LORD, O my soul,
>> and all that is within me, bless his holy Name.
> Bless the LORD, O my soul,
>> and forget not all his benefits.
> He forgives all your sins
>> and heals all your infirmities;
> He redeems your life from the grave
>> and crowns you with mercy and loving-kindness.
>> Psalm 103:1–4

Years later, the hospital has become a not unfamiliar place to me. It no longer bears quite the same fright for me as it once did. Sometimes it has been a refuge, and sometimes a place to rest. But it is always humbling because I have seen others who suffer as much and even more than I. I never would have thought such a thing was possible. Do not shun hospitalization if you are ill. It is God's castle to keep us safe.

Neither should one reject ECT as a possible treatment if a doctor whom you trust recommends it. Although I had terrible problems with my memory after one of my series of treatments, for the most part they dissipated. The important thing is that it can relieve the worst of the symptoms and return some degree of normalcy to the patient's life. I would not hesitate to have ECT if my medications start to fail again. ECT can be an almost immediate lifesaver.

Another type of therapy I was blessed with that spring was an outpatient program at the Institute of Living (IOL) at Hartford Hospital. This was more help than anything, except maybe ECT. Yale Psychiatric Institute was a safe place for me to be, a sort of holding tank, until I could get well enough to go back to my life. But the Professionals Program at the Institute of Living used what is called cognitive behavioral therapy (CBT). This involves a structured attempt at changing negative thought patterns, such as feelings of failure and self-loathing that become habits while one is mentally ill. I spent five weeks in the intensive outpatient program there.

It was a "day program" for professionals. We were teachers, priests, insurance executives, and nuns. We spent the hours of 9:00 to 2:00, Monday through Friday, in intensive group therapy. We had a lot of opportunity for talk therapy. They even had a "gym" program. I have hated gym ever since childhood, and I didn't really like gym at the IOL either, but it was among the most memorable of activities in the program. We were made to play the types of games one plays in youth group: cooperative, noncompetitive, interactive. This meant that we all had to work together on a task or toward a goal. Even participating in these activities, as annoying as they were (who wants to be in youth group again?), was healing. As a team, we could in fact accomplish tasks. We found, surprisingly, that we were not a group of failures.

The companionship there was healing in itself. Even though by this point I could realize that darkness was not in fact my only companion, I still felt mightily alone. No one knew how I was really feeling except my therapist. I was still trying to hide it—even from my husband. I was still ashamed of my illness. I was still ashamed that I could not rejoice even at the greatest, or even at the smallest, of God's gifts. But at the IOL, I interacted with people who felt the same way I did. We all were despairing of the future, unable to make decisions, feeling like complete failures. And that some of the others were religious leaders also meant a lot to me. The loneliness of mental illness only perpetuates its symptoms, but at the IOL I realized that I was not alone even in my illness.

I therefore think that, in the pit of mental illness, one should not avoid medications, psychiatrists, hospitals, even ECT. It is true that Christians and non-Christians alike may fear these therapies. I have known people who have been quite frankly sick unto death who nevertheless refuse this kind of help out of fear. I will look at this further in chapter 13.

Ultimately, the hospital broke down my impressions of myself as strong. I had to admit that I was weak. This, for the Christian, can be an important spiritual lesson that can be learned anywhere, but I happened to learn it under the cover of a place that kept me safe from myself. Being on a locked unit was humiliating. But the Christian needs to remember Jesus's words that everyone who exalts herself will be humbled, and everyone who humbles herself will be exalted (Luke 14:11). Maybe I just needed to be humbled that I could know the exaltation of Christ in a new way. But the hospital was a place of healing for me, where Christ entered into and pushed back my darkness.

> They will hunger no more, and thirst no more;
>   the sun will not strike them,
>   nor any scorching heat;
> for the Lamb at the center of the throne will be their
>   shepherd,
>   and he will guide them to springs of the water of life,
>   and God will wipe away every tear from their eyes.
>   Revelation 7:16–17

PART TWO

Faith and Mental Illness

7

Feeling, Memory, and Personality

You have given so much to me, give one thing more—a grateful heart.

George Herbert (1593–1633)

Karl Barth, a Swiss Reformed theologian of the twentieth century, once said that the creaturely counterpart to the grace of God is gratitude. Is it possible for the depressed soul to be grateful? If not, does this mean that people living with mental illnesses cannot respond to God in creaturely counterpart? What would it look like, what would it mean, for a heart that is cast down to be lifted up in gratitude to God? Sometimes I think the only way for me to be grateful is to pray the Psalms. To pray the prayers of Israel. To wrap my tongue around the gracious words of those before me in the faith, in hopes that their words will nourish my soul, somehow sink in and sprout into trees of righteousness, burst into songs of hope. Because I have no words of gratitude in me, only horror and shame at my absolute hardness of heart.

> Of all the miseries that people experience, sickness is greater than any of them. It is the immediate sword of God. . . . In poverty I lack things and in banishment I lack the company of other people, but in sickness I lack myself.
>
> John Donne (1572–1631)

Sometimes the only thing one can do is to hold on to this hope: that one will praise God once again. "Hope in God; for I shall again praise him, my help and my God" (Ps. 42:5 NRSV). Hope involves memory, not only of the past but also a "memory" of the future. A memory of the promise that the future redemption of Israel will become present in our own lives. This means that memory is such a vitally important part of spiritual health. When one is depressed, memory can fill in the gaps that the inability to feel has left vacant. One may not be able to feel God's grace, but one may be able to remember it. There is profound wisdom in the biblical injunction to write the narrative of God's redemption on your doorposts, to talk of it when you sit and when you walk, and when you lie down and when you rise up. Remind yourself always of God's election and love for us (Deut. 6:4–9; cf. 11:18–21). In all of the details of life, remind yourself of God's redemption, and the memory of that redemption past and future will carry you through the times when you can't feel.

This is why it is so important to worship in community, to ask your brothers and sisters in Christ to pray for you, and to pray with them. Sometimes you literally cannot pray on your own, and you need to borrow from the faith of those around you. Sometimes I cannot even recite the creed unless I am doing it in the context of worship, along with all the body of Christ. Now, you could say that this is a failure of cognition and memory from the symptoms, the ECT, and the medications. It is that in part, but I think it goes further than that. When reciting the creed, I borrow from the recitation of others. Companionship in the Lord Jesus is powerful.

The story of the paralytic in Mark 2 demonstrates this. The man's friends are determined to have Jesus heal him, so they rip apart the roof and lower their friend down on his bed to Jesus. "When Jesus saw *their* faith, he said to the paralytic, 'Son, your sins are forgiven.'" The faith of the friends here is crucial for the paralytic's healing. I have borrowed from the faithfulness of the community, the body of Christ, and I believe that the faith of my community has been crucial for my own healing. One blessing that we can hope to wrestle out of God in this Jacob-like struggle is that we may at daybreak finally learn what grace really is.

Depression and madness? I am coming to see that when most people talk about depression, they are not talking about what I experience. And it is so hard to talk about. I don't want to sound like this is some kind of a competition. But I am not talking about down-in-the-dumps grumps. That is not madness, I agree. But when major depression gets truly bad, it is indeed like madness. The personality seems to dissolve. Tastes, desires, dispositions that formerly marked one's "self" can disappear in a depression. Will I ever be me again, and if so, what will that "me" be on the other side of this madness? So what does this mean? What does this mean before God that the personality should seem to dry up and be born away on the wind? I suppose it means that the personality is relatively unimportant vis-à-vis God. In God's eyes we are not defined by how we feel, by what we think, even by what we do. We are what God does with us. And what God does with us is to save us from our best yet perverse efforts to separate ourselves from his presence, from his fellowship, communion, sharing.

Of course, saying that the personality is not very important is not acceptable in much of the Christian world these days, to say the least. I find that many people think of God as a self-help device we can use to improve our personality. To help us quit smoking, drinking, overeating. To help us be nicer people so we can stand to live in our own skin. To help us win more friends and influence more people. Or maybe even to be more affluent. The drive to improve ourselves, personality included, motivates much religion in America. Many of us Christians are functional atheists, even though we may be quite pious indeed. We often can't imagine how our religion would require anything of us that would not be directed solely to our own betterment. Even working toward justice and peace can sometimes be a veiled attempt to make us feel less unacceptable to ourselves, easier to live with. But if God is really the God of the Bible, then he demands our worship and obedience despite how we feel about it, or about ourselves, or others. Of course, it is always pleasant to feel good. And it would be especially nice not to go through life wanting to end it. But even this doesn't separate us from God. Even wanting to return the gift of life does not damn us. "God proves his love for us in that while we were still sinners Christ died for us" (Rom. 5:8). Even before we make the slightest move out of our sloth to reach out to God this is true. The hard part when one is mentally ill can be choosing life. It is ever that, though, which is demanded of us. This is the hard part. How we feel does not change anything objectively about our life before God.

What will allow for our survival is not how we feel but what we remember, what God did for us and does for us. The Ba'al Shem Tov (1698–1760, founder of the Hasidic movement in Judaism) once said, "Exile is caused by forgetfulness, and the secret of redemption is memory." I must remember, even if I don't feel it, that I am part of a people of faith, of hope, of love. I cannot doubt or question that memory, even though all evidence would lead me to conclude that I never really did trust, never really did hope, never really did love. I may feel like a hypocrite now for even pretending to pray. But how I feel, after all, is not that important. If I can do nothing else, I must simply remember that I am a part of the community of faith, the body of Christ, that I was once able to participate in the praises of Israel. "Put your trust in God; for I will yet give thanks to him, who is the help of my countenance, and my God" (Ps. 42:7). That will sustain us, and it may be all that sustains us. Remembering the past anchors hope for the future. It may not change how we feel in the present moment, but surely it will help us to endure.

> Hear O Israel: The LORD is our God, the LORD alone. You shall love the LORD your God with all your heart, and with all your soul, and with all your might. Keep these words that I am commanding you today in your heart. Recite them to your children and talk about them when you are at home and when you are away, when you lie down and when you rise.
>
> Deuteronomy 6:4–7

Thus has Israel remembered the glories of its God, his gifts, his mercies, his leading. Israel remembers the past and thereby allows God to build a future for and among them. Without the memories of God's past with Israel, Israel has no reason for present strength or future hope.

If it is true that memory of the past serves not so much to preserve the past as to create a present for us and to reach out to the future, what does it mean when we are not able to remember? What of the person who physically can no longer remember? Is this a disadvantage to the soul? David Keck writes movingly of his mother's illness with Alzheimer's in his book *Forgetting Whose We Are*. This is exactly the tragedy: we cannot remember and so we lose track of whose we are. Objectively, of course, our identity in Christ remains ever the same: beloved and redeemed. But forgetfulness deprives our consciousness of this knowledge and with it of its solace. The great tragedy of this is the break in relationships: here again, past affects present and future.

So my own memories should give me hope. The New Testament memories of the resurrection of Jesus should give me a past, present, and future—just as we proclaim the mystery of faith in our liturgy, "Christ has died, Christ is risen, Christ will come again." God's past faithfulness to me should undergird and shield me from my despair. Does it? Only when I am able to absorb these acts of faithful care into my memory. But sometimes my memory is compromised by the medication, by the ECT, and by the illness itself. With hope this will get better soon.

After the first series of ECT treatments, I was unable to remember much at all. I could not remember my bank codes, my phone number, the kind of car I drove. This made finding my car in the parking lot doubly difficult. Not only did I forget where I had left it, but I also forgot what it was that I had left. What did it look like? What was the make and model, the color and shape of my car? I forgot the details of the books I had written, even the outline of the story of Israel and the New Testament. It was so bad that I had to cancel speaking engagements, and in a job interview I so thoroughly forgot even the subject matter of my dissertation that I made a complete fool of myself. Needless to say, I did not get that job. I am sure the interviewers thought I was a lame case, overrated by my professors.

I had to have an IQ test in preparation for being admitted to the ordination process in the Episcopal Church. The psychologist examining me proclaimed with an almost triumphant smile on his face that my IQ was in the low sixties (the average being one hundred). Never mind that I have three graduate degrees from an Ivy League university. I simply could not fathom how to put a set of blocks together to make the shapes indicated on the paper templates. I could not remember from second to second what I was doing, nor could I discern each future step in the process. My shame at that event was surpassed only by the psychologist's telling me next that I would not be passed on to the bishop with recommendation for ordination. I thank God for my bishop's understanding and willingness to look beyond the obvious symptoms. He, at least, understood that mental illness is just that: an illness that can be managed with the proper care.

Throughout the Bible we see the importance of memory, of memorizing, of remembering. "My soul is heavy within me; therefore I will remember you from the land of Jordan, and from the peak of Mizar among the heights of Hermon" (Ps. 42:8 [NRSV

42:6]). The heaviness of the soul is lessened by the remembrance of concrete places and acts God has done. "Why are you so full of heaviness, O my soul? and why are you so disquieted within me?" (42:6 [NRSV 42:5]). Memory of God's mercies brings us from heaviness to thanksgiving, the biblical model of health.

The same is true of form in the liturgy: we can memorize the prayers, the collects, the creed, so that they come back to us throughout the week to nourish our soul. But even that is denied someone whose memory is compromised. At times when ill, I would reach for the words of collects and prayers and be left with a blank. For people with intact memory, the forms of the liturgy themselves are like memories that reach to the past, establish the present, and secure hope in the future. Denominations that do not have a prayer book can lack this, although their hymnals sometimes serve this purpose. However, when congregations tend to reinvent their forms of worship every week, the internalization and memorizing is of a different order. I think of the difference between J. S. Bach and John Cage: Bach used existing forms and composed broadly. Cage had to invent his own forms, and therefore left fewer than one-tenth the number of Bach's compositions. The liturgy sinks into our soul and can come back in time of need in its forms through our memory.

Ironically, forgetfulness can be all one wants when profoundly depressed. In a hypomanic state, before it turns into a nightmare, one is so elated as not to think about memory. Who cares about anything but the present in hypomania? This is part of the problem. This is at the root of the excesses of mania: one cannot even imagine a time when today's actions may become tomorrow's curse. But when depressed, one wants simply to be unaware of the present which causes such pain. What is deemed good by a healthy person is despised by the sick. This is an example of the perversity of the symptoms of mental illness. This is part of what distinguishes mental anguish from physical pain. The very thing that could aid in healing is often shunned by the mentally ill, whereas the physically ill usually want their health to improve.

As a deer longs for the water-brooks,
    so longs my soul for you, O God.
My soul is athirst for God, athirst for the living God;
    when shall I come to appear before the presence of
        God?
My tears have been my food day and night,
    while all day they say to me,
    "Where now is your God?"
I pour out my soul when I think on these things:
    how I went with the multitude and led them into the
        house of God,
With the voice of praise and thanksgiving,
    among those who keep holy-day.
Why are you so full of heaviness, O my soul?
    and why are you so disquieted within me?
Put your trust in God;
    for I will yet give thanks to him,
    who is the help of my countenance, and my God.

                          Psalm 42:1–7 [42:1–6]

In the midst of an impenetrable depression, one is often unable to sense the presence of God at all. Sometimes all one can feel is the complete absence of God, one's utter abandonment by God, the ridiculousness of the very notion of a loving and merciful God. This cuts to the heart of the Christian and challenges everything she believes about the world and about herself. But if one is depressed, one should not expect to feel otherwise. In fact, feeling is not really that important for the life of faith.

Ever since Friedrich Schleiermacher (1768–1834) defined religion as the feeling of absolute dependence, Christians in the Protestant West have tended to follow suit. Religion is often framed in terms of feeling or experience. And so G. W. F. Hegel (1770–1831) quipped that if Christianity were the feeling of absolute dependence, his dog would be the best Christian he ever knew. If we really thought that feeling is the essence of the Christian faith, the depressed Christian would be given all the more ammunition for self-destruction.

Since she cannot by definition feel anything but violence toward and hatred of the self, and if that "feeling" were to be validated as religiously significant, why should she bother pushing away the desire for self-annihilation? Often we simply cannot change the way we feel. Despair, abandonment, isolation, and meaninglessness are sometimes unavoidable, and sheer endurance is the only way to deal with them. It is a good thing, then, that God does not look upon us according to our feelings but according to the faithfulness of Jesus Christ.

Of course, feelings and their examination are key in the work of psychotherapy. I am not denying the importance of being honest with one's feelings in psychotherapy for the health of the mind, and maybe also even the soul. I am simply questioning the religious significance of feelings, especially for the Christian religion, in the economy of salvation. Our salvation is something Jesus wrought on the cross, not in the interiority of our personality. When our personality frays under the strain of mental illness, this does not mean that God regards our soul any differently from when we are mentally healthy.

8

Brain, Mind, and Soul

The soul that to Jesus hath fled for repose,
I will not, I will not desert to its foes;
That soul, though all hell should endeavor to shake,
I'll never, no never, no never forsake.

John Rippon (1751–1836)

According to the Smithsonian Institution, the brain makes up only 2 percent of the body's weight but uses 20 percent of the body's fuel. Such a miracle. But my "enemy," in the psalmist's terms, has been my brain itself. The gray matter inside my skull. The physical organ without which I could not live, without which I would have no functioning mind. But what is the mind? It seems to be more than the brain. It seems to serve as seat of the intellect, a sort of intermediary between the brain and the world of ideas and social interaction. It is the mind that may or may not apprehend God as an intellectual idea or problem.

What is, then, the relation between the brain and the soul? Is it similar to the relation between the brain and the mind? Does the soul equal the mind, as the capacity for consciousness and memory? If the brain is the biological organ itself, and the mind is the seat of consciousness, memory, and the capacity for social engagement, the soul might be seen as the whole person, the self, through which we have communion with God. While it may take the mind to apprehend God as a "problem," it takes the soul to love and cleave to God as Holy Trinity.

Of course, seeing these as three distinct items—brain, mind, and soul—even if inseparable, is odd. Some think of the mind as merely the functioning brain. The soul, if it is acknowledged at all, is merely a faculty of the mind. One analogy I have heard: the brain is like the TV set, and the mind is like the functioning of the TV set. What then is the soul?

I am not interested here in the ancient question and its traditional answers regarding the relation between the soul and the body as two separate entities. It is clear from biblical teaching, especially from the Old Testament, that the soul and body are united, however we choose to talk about that. We are created body and soul in the image of the triune God. Certainly the resurrected body will be different from our earthly body (1 Cor. 15:35–55). But that the soul and body are one is assumed in Scripture. This is also assumed in the words at the distribution of the elements at the eucharist: "The body/blood of our Lord Jesus Christ, given for you, preserve your *body and soul* unto everlasting life." We are a unity: body and soul.

I am more interested at the moment in the specific relation between the brain, the mind, and the soul in mental illness. One could say that the same questions arise in relation to any kind of physical suffering. That may be true, but in the suffering of mental illness the brain and mind play a unique role. I want to suggest that while it is true that the brain of a mentally ill person is in fact ill, the illness of the soul does not necessarily follow.

After I had my first round of ECT, I underwent an MRI (magnetic resonance imaging) of my brain. I was given a mild anesthetic and then trundled into a coffinlike tube, where I had to remain very still for far too long while the machine whirred and clanked around me. The ECT treatments had left me so disoriented that the doctor wanted to make sure there was nothing anatomically wrong with my brain, such as a tumor. I was fine, of course—or rather, I was in an agony of confusion but had no tumor.

I have seen since then that PET (positron emission tomography) scans can show the different structures of the brain in mental health and in mental illness. PET scans are used for research, not for diagnosis, but they do indicate that mental illnesses are physical events. The actual structures of the brain appear different, some withered, some enlarged, when the brain is ill. The biological model for understanding mental illnesses as physical events is not simply a way to apologize for an array of difficult symptoms. To take only one of the illnesses, Major Depression is clearly a physical event. But it does not end there. It carries with it spiritual side effects.

The redeemed soul longs for God. This is part of the soul's function: to reach out to its Creator, to seek and to be sought by God. The fallen soul naturally longs for created things in place of the Creator. The Christian, caught between the desires for the transient and the eternal, longs for both God's creation and the Creator. Depression may intensify the soul's longing for God, since the disease can make the created order seem so despicable. Depression can in a counterintuitive sense be a good, or at least it can render good insofar as the soul's thirst for God may be increased. This was true in my case.

Since only God is the source of all healing, it is appropriate that the Christian soul sometimes searches for God more in illness than in health. But the soul reaches out and often cannot find God. Depression increases our longing for the One who heals, yet the disease veils our view of him. "We were made for Thee and our hearts are restless until they rest in Thee" (Augustine). This is true of the human soul, according to Augustine. I find that it is even moreso for the Christian who lives with Major Depression. The jewels of the world never fill the soul—and in mental illness, for the Christian, this is more agonizingly the case. Nothing in the world satisfies, but the longing is intensified. All becomes a seeking for God, for God's blessing and God's comfort. Yet even while this longing is intensified, the object of its desire is painfully removed from view. The soul thirsts for God and yet is pushed further away from the source of its slaking.

> The whole round world is not enough to fill
> The heart's three corners, but it craveth still:
> None but the Trinity, who made it, can
> Suffice the vast triangulated heart of man.
>   Christopher Harvey (1597–1663)

Adam is created from the dust, and God breathes into his nostrils the breath of life, and the man becomes a "living being" (*nephesh hayah*: living soul, Gen. 2:7). He does not have a soul; he *is* soul, an ensouled body and an embodied soul. Along with the body, the soul is the totality of the human creature: brain, mind, feelings, actions, inclinations, desires, and life. All of these aspects affect the soul, but they do not add up to the soul. Since God is the One who shapes the soul, calls it, imprints it with his image, and sends it out as witness to his grace in the world, the soul cannot be simply a collection of the functions of the human mind. Since the triune God is himself being-in-relation, to be created in the image of this God is to be ensouled body, and this means to be in relation to all creation.

Mental illness breaks this continuum of relationship, since in severe mental illness the sufferer is often rendered virtually unable to relate. Mental illness threatens to turn us in upon ourselves. It does not necessarily destroy the relational continuum, unless the sufferer should commit the final act of negation of all relation by committing suicide.

Mental illness can potentially damage the soul, since it preys on the brain and the mind, but it cannot *destroy* the soul. God holds the soul in his hands. What does this mean for suicides, who destroy their own body? Our relation to the triune God cannot end simply by the act of suicide. We have heard it said that God's yes is greater than our no. Our rejection of God, of ourselves, of our lives, is not greater than God. Even though suicide is clearly a final separation from one's fellow creatures, it is not moreso than natural death would be. And natural death does not stop God from loving the soul, or the soul from loving God.

> Eternal and most glorious God, you have stamped the soul of humanity with your Image, received it into your revenue, and made it part of your treasure; do not allow us so to undervalue ourselves, so to impoverish you, as to give away these souls for nothing, and all the world is nothing if the soul must be given for it. Do this, O God, for his sake who knows our natural infirmities, for he had them, and knows the weight of our sins, for he paid a dear price for them; your Son, our Savior Jesus Christ.
>
> John Donne (1572–1631)

This view of the soul has implications for how the church treats suicides. If I am right and suicide does not ultimately separate the soul of the Christian from God, then why would we have moral difficulties giving suicides a Christian burial? Why would we be reticent to comfort the families left in the wake of a suicide? A baptized Christian remains a Christian. Possibly the difficulty lies in the horror and shame of the suicide. She is outcast in death because she could not live, because she was not able to go on living. Her rejection of life is perceived as a failure on the part of the suicide, the family, and the church. Historically more significant is the understanding that the act of suicide is a transgression of the commandment not to murder. To live is therefore an act of obedience to God.

What does this mean for my own illness? Most of the time when I was ill, I was unable consciously to witness to the grace of God. Or at least so I felt. Even then my sermons were still greeted with appreciation by my parish. Maybe they were just being kind.

If my feelings were dead vis-à-vis God, this does not mean that my soul was sick. My brain certainly was sick, and my mind was sick, but God held my soul firmly throughout, keeping me longing for him—even though it felt to me as if I had been abandoned. Abandonment, however, is not God's way of operating except at the moment of Christ's crucifixion.

Is the soul different, then, from the heart or the spirit? These latter words are both biblical terms that are used in tandem with *soul*. "You shall love the Lord your God with all your heart, and with all your soul, and with all your strength, and with all your mind, and your neighbor as yourself" (Luke 10:27; cf. Lev. 19:18; Deut. 6:5). *Heart*, *soul*, and *mind* are not three distinct faculties but different biblical terms that designate the very being of the person.

Another way of looking at the soul, from one purely scientific view, is that we are all animal, and the "soul" is simply the brain. In this view, our personhood can be seen in consciousness, love, friendship, and morality.[1] But if this is so, we are basically all animal, since the soul itself is equated with the brain. Certainly the Christian tradition does teach that humanity is animal, created on the same day as land animals. But the Christian tradition also teaches that human beings were created in God's image and given a special blessing and task beyond that given to the animals (Gen. 1:28–30).

Another way of looking at the soul is to let it answer the question of the central *whatness* of humanity. Descartes's "I think, therefore I am" functioned to answer the *whatness* of humanity with our capacity to reason. What can be said about human *whatness* with regard to the mentally ill? When I was ill, cognition was slowed and reasoning became terribly difficult. At times it was impossible. Shall I then say that "I was not"? It certainly felt that way, but as I have said, feelings are untrustworthy in one's relationship to God. Maybe an affirmation more central to the *whatness* of humanity would be "I love, therefore I am." According to Scripture, love brings us into the very ground and source of our being, the love of God. The objective nature of God's love for me was what brought me through the darkness and kept me from giving up on myself and all those around me.

But the mentally ill sometimes cannot love aright. Consider the mother in Texas who on November 24, 2004, severed the arms from her eight-month-old daughter, killing her. A mother is supposed to love and protect her child. What then of this woman's humanity? What of her soul? Because of God's love for her, her soul could have still been healthy, even though the brain and mind were desperately sickened. This mother's own love for God may have been compromised by her actions and her mental life, but it is God alone who holds that desperate mother's soul in life.

What makes the soul and therefore the human is God's love, not the soul's love for anything else. Therefore we might best say that the *whatness* of humanity is "I *am loved*, therefore I am." This is in part what the Christian tradition means by the creation of humanity by God: the soul is loved into existence by God.

What is the relation between our consciousness, feelings, thoughts, desires—that is, our mental life—and our brain and our soul? First of all, we see by the mere existence of feelings, thoughts, and desires that our mind is more than just a brain. The brain is the physical organ that allows the function of the mind, and of the body for that matter. Because the image of God is in us, we can see that the soul is more than both of these combined. The soul is not the sum of the parts of the nonphysical, because it is created by God and sustained by God. This createdness gives the soul an objectivity beyond the merely nonphysical aspects of "me."

Notice what I am *not* saying. One philosopher compares the soul to a light bulb and the brain to the socket into which the soul is "plugged." The soul will "function (have a mental life) if it is plugged into a functioning brain."[2] The implication is that the soul's function is to have a mental life. If that were so, mentally ill people would have sick souls, since their mental life is indeed compromised, but this is not consistent with a biblical understanding of the soul. As I have said, the function of the soul is to witness to the image of God and to reach out for God in praise

and thanksgiving. Instead of the light bulb analogy, which understands the sick soul to be associated with a sick brain, I would
suggest that the sick soul is the soul of the person who does not
acknowledge the image of God in herself. This lack of acknowl-
edgment may have something to do with mental illness, but it may
not. It may have to do with despising God, or simply not knowing
enough about God to understand what acknowledging that image
would mean. It is those who do not return thanks to God who are
soul-sick, not necessarily those who suffer from mental illness.

What then does all of this mean for the mentally ill? When love,
friendship, and even morality (especially in cases of suicide and
murder) are brought into question, does this mean that the soul
itself is impaired or injured? For the Christian tradition, the meaningful life is not based on our human desires or our consciousness
but on our relationship to the God of Israel, the triune God who
endows our lives with meaning. And that relationship is wrought
in the life, death, and resurrection of Jesus. The soul is not the seat
of sickness in the mentally ill. The brain is broken: its synapses and
neurons and receptors. At least for the time being. But the soul,
as the self in relation to God, continues healthy in anyone as long
as that person is in Christ, relating to and acknowledging God.

> The soul that to Jesus hath fled for repose,
> I will not, I will not desert to its foes.

9

Sin, Suffering, and Despair

> Lord God, almighty and everlasting Father, you have
> brought us in safety to this new day: Preserve us with
> your mighty power, that we may not fall into sin, nor be
> overcome by adversity; and in all that we do, direct us
> to the fulfilling of your purpose, through Jesus Christ
> our Lord. Amen.
>
> BCP, 137

What is the relationship between suffering in mental illness and
sin? Is mental illness caused by sin, or is it in some way a punishment for sin? On the one hand I would say no, that does not
sound worthy of God. And yet of course we suffer because of our
sins of commission and omission all the time. The psalmist says,

> There is no health in my flesh
> because of your indignation;
>   there is no soundness in my body, because of my sin.
> For my iniquities overwhelm me;
>   like a heavy burden they are too much for me to bear.
>
> Psalm 38:3–4

101

How can this be so? Is it really true that I am sick because of my misdeeds toward God and neighbor? Like a heavy burden, this thought is too much for me to bear. Here is an example, from the prayer book of Israel, of what mental illness can feel like when God's wrath is the cause.[1]

> LORD, do not rebuke me in your anger;
>   do not punish me in your wrath.
> Have pity on me, LORD, for I am weak;
>   heal me, LORD, for my bones are racked.
> My spirit shakes with terror;
>   how long, O LORD, how long?
> Turn, O LORD, and deliver me;
>   save me for your mercy's sake.
> For in death no one remembers you;
>   and who will give you thanks in the grave?
> I grow weary because of my moaning;
>   every night I drench my bed
>   and flood my couch with tears.
> My eyes are wasted away with grief
>   and worn because of all my enemies.
> Depart from me, all evildoers,
>   for the LORD has heard the sound of my weeping.
> The LORD has heard my supplication;
>   the LORD accepts my prayer.
> All my enemies shall be confounded and quake with fear;
>   they shall turn back and suddenly be put to shame.
>
>   Psalm 6

Here the psalmist understands his own suffering as a result of the anger of God. Such an understanding of the wrath of God is exceedingly unpopular in our culture. We prefer to see God as nice, indeed rather innocuous. But notice that these words in a sense comfort the psalmist: "LORD, do not rebuke me in your anger!" The psalmist is allowed to ask for God's mercy. At least we know that there is a cause of the suffering. It is not random or ill-placed. It is because of God's anger. This is not so, for example, for William Styron: "The pain is unrelenting, and what makes the condition intolerable is the foreknowledge that no remedy will come—not in a day, an hour, a month, or a minute." Styron's suffering is meaningless, whereas the psalmist is drawn into relationship with God in his suffering.

And there is a way out of this situation for the psalmist, while there is no way out of random suffering: "Do not punish me in your wrath!" God listens to the prayers of his people and takes pity. Otherwise there would be no point for the psalmist to make a plea: "Have pity on me, LORD, for I am weak!" The psalmist even pleads with God, making a deal: you must not let me die, because if you did, you would only have one less mouth to praise you! At the end of the psalm, the LORD has heard the prayer of the psalmist, and the psalmist gloats over his enemies, who will be confounded. It would not be inappropriate to read the enemies here as the symptoms a mentally ill person might have. These symptoms are certainly enemies, and they shall be turned back, according to the psalm. The psalmist's cry turns to a shout of joy and hope, not because of any inner reflection or reasoning, but because "the LORD has heard the sound of my weeping."

Notice how diffcrent the psalm is from the descriptions of mental illness by modern authors. The psalmist cries out in pain ("I . . . flood my couch with tears") and exhibits symptoms ("my eyes are wasted with grief"). But a psalm is more than just a lament: it grounds both its lament and its trust on the faithfulness of God to bring healing. Can we not understand healing to come from God in the way the psalmist says ("the LORD accepts my prayer")?

<hr/>

When evening had come, he said to them, "Let us go across to the other side." And leaving the crowd behind, they took him with them in the boat, just as he was. Other boats were with him. A great windstorm arose, and the waves beat into the boat, so that the boat was already being swamped. But he was in the stern, asleep

on the cushion; and they woke him up and said to him, "Teacher,
do you not care that we are perishing?"

Mark 4:35–38

Teacher, do you not care that I am perishing? Do you not see that
the waves are already overtaking my boat? Do you sleep? The One
who watches over Israel shall neither slumber nor sleep: are you
really that Good Shepherd?

> He woke up and rebuked the wind, and said to the sea, "Peace! Be
> still!" Then the wind ceased, and there was a dead calm. He said
> to them, "Why are you afraid? Have you still no faith?" And they
> were filled with great awe and said to one another, "Who then is
> this, that even the wind and the sea obey him?"

Mark 4:39–41

Rebuke the wind, calm the waves, still the chaos within. You who
were present at the creation of the world, within the very bosom
of God the Father, you who at creation calmed the stormy chaos
of the waters by creating the land, the dry land on which humanity is to live, protected from the waters of destruction, dear Word
of God, in me create islands of peace, footholds in the midst of
the raging sea.

Grant, dear Lord, that I may again be of use to you, to teach
your law and your grace. Clear my thoughts, calm my thinking,
dwell in my heart as its only Teacher and Guide.

～～～

> They came to the other side of the sea, to the country of the Ger-
> asenes. And when he had stepped out of the boat, immediately
> a man out of the tombs with an unclean spirit met him. He lived
> among the tombs; and no one could restrain him any more, even
> with a chain; for he had often been restrained with shackles and
> chains, but the chains he wrenched apart, and the shackles he broke
> in pieces; and no one had the strength to subdue him. Night and day
> among the tombs and on the mountains he was always howling and

bruising himself with stones. When he saw Jesus from a distance, he ran and bowed down before him; and he shouted at the top of his voice, "What have you to do with me, Jesus, Son of the Most High God? I adjure you by God, do not torment me." For he had said to him, "Come out of the man, you unclean spirit!" Then Jesus asked him, "What is your name?" He replied, "My name is Legion; for we are many." He begged him earnestly not to send them out of the country.

Mark 5:1–10

We are legion. But we are usually invisible to the naked eye. We look as if we are human, even though the human is merely the host for our banquet, the silent devouring of flesh and guzzling of blood. Parasitic. We make our hosts walk among the living as though dead, and most of the time the living cannot recognize that we are survivors within the dying host.

Until we make our host so sick that she would choose tombs for a dwelling that she needs to be bound by chains. And especially when even the chains cannot bind our host, the living see just how much we have sucked the life out of her. But usually all they see is the host, and they blame the host, as if she had choice in the matter of having demons plague her. So the living are often just as happy to slough off the host and force her to dwell among the tombs.

At such a point, it is Jesus who has the power to bind our diseases, for he is the Strong Man. He knows that our disease, our demons, are separate from us. To the ill, the disease seems to take over, until one is entirely an illness. Jesus knows this is not true, and he can cast out the demons without destroying us. Only he can cast out of us our impurity, our uncleanness, our illnesses. Only he can cast the demons out from us into the pigs, then into the sea. Impurity dwelling among the impure is cast into the impure and then herded into the chaos.

The thing is that the man's demons don't want to go away, don't want to be cast out. It is easier to dwell where you are than to allow Jesus to root you out, even if you are in the cemetery, living among the walking dead.

> Blessed be the God and Father of our Lord Jesus Christ! By his great mercy he has given us a new birth into a living hope through the resurrection of Jesus Christ from the dead.
>
> 1 Peter 1:3

This story about the demoniac living among the tombs functions somewhat like the passion predictions later in Mark 8:30, 9:30, and 10:33–34. But here the passion is illustrated rather than stated, in the form of a miracle story, somewhat like the story of the raising of Lazarus in John's Gospel. Here Jesus conquers the legion of demons, clothing the man in his right mind, giving him new life, and restoring him to community among the living.

And how this disturbs the swineherds. Resurrection sticks in the throat, not only for the demons, but for all who deal with and pander in impurity. We await the day when we may regain the peace of Adam and Eve, who were "naked and not ashamed," when we will be fully clothed in the power of the resurrection. *By his great mercy he has given us a new birth into a living hope through the resurrection of Jesus Christ from the dead* (1 Pet. 1:3).

To speak of the mentally ill and demons in the same breath can be truly offensive to those who live with such brain disorders—especially if mental illness is *equated with* demon possession and vice versa. Mental illnesses are generally understood these days to be biologically and socially caused, not spiritually based. But these illnesses do have spiritual fallout. And the Christian knows that the Strong Man who will bind this spiritual fallout is Jesus. For this we who live among so many tombs do have hope. But we have to remember that. And we have to pray, although that may seem impossible while our symptoms flare.

> The LORD's arm is not too short to save,
>   nor his ear too dull to hear.

> Rather, your iniquities have been barriers
>   between you and your God,
> and your sins have hidden his face from you
>   so that he does not hear.
>
> Isaiah 59:1–2

This is a hard saying. It is my iniquities that raise a barrier between me and God? Because of my sins God hides his face from
me? Now this would never go over well with my psychiatrist. Any
relation of my illness and guilt before God would be quickly swept
away at best, and openly confronted and rejected at worst. But
how am I to read this? Yes, of course, it was the chosen people's
iniquities that caused God in Isaiah's time to turn a deaf ear. What
sins have I that God would turn his face from me? How are my
sins any different from others' sins, that I myself would be stuck
with this awful disease? My doctors and therapists would never
want me to say this bipolar disorder is my fault. Neither would
I. Isaiah and other writers throughout the Bible do link suffering
and disaster with sin.

The challenge is placed for me therefore to look to my own heart
and see if this is the case for me. Maybe my doctors would look
at the question this way: to what extent do your desires and fears
and actions trip you up so as to let mental illness gain a foothold?
Maybe where they would say desires, I would say misplaced desires;
where they would say fears, I would say faithless fears; where they
would say actions, I would say disobedient acts. But they would
probably not even go this far. They would say that mental illness
is a biological problem exacerbated by stress in one's life. Period.
And I believe that, so far as it goes.

But I as a Christian must struggle with the question of sin. How
does my disobedience to God cause me to suffer? More important, how does the Christian understand sin? My sin is manifest
in my many little misdeeds, and even big ones, but the power that
separates us from God is greater than these. This power makes
us commit our little (and large) acts of disobedience. This power

makes us omit obedience. This power, like a force field around us,
is overcome by the power of the cross and resurrection, a force far
greater than that of sin.

> LORD, be merciful to me;
>   heal me, for I have sinned against you.
>   Psalm 41:4

Then again, in John 9, at the healing of the man born blind,
it is the disciples themselves who ask, "Rabbi, who sinned, this
man or his parents, that he was born blind?" Jesus answered that
neither the man born blind nor his parents had sinned, but rather
he was born blind so that God's works might be revealed in him.
Can this illness in me show God's works? That would make it all
worth it to me. As G. K. Chesterton (1874–1936) once said, "One
sees great things from the valley, only small things from the peak."
Perhaps God has thrust me into this valley that I might see his
great mountain from its foot.

From the valley of depression one does see more than from the
peaks of hypomania, or even from the peaks of "normal" happiness. Why does my illness give me wisdom? Do I want this kind
of wisdom, born of so much suffering?

> Surely he has borne our griefs
>   and carried our sorrows;
> yet we esteemed him stricken,
>   smitten by God, and afflicted.
> But he was wounded for our transgressions,
>   he was bruised for our iniquities;
> upon him was the chastisement that made us whole,
>   and with his stripes we are healed.
> All we like sheep have gone astray,
>   we have turned every one to his own way;
> and the LORD has laid on him
>   the iniquity of us all.
>   Isaiah 53:4–6 RSV

Does the LORD lay on Jesus the iniquity of us all? Can I say that my sins are borne away in the shadow of his wings? Why then do I continue to suffer? Have I just turned astray, like the lost sheep? Is this all my fault?

> As a door turns on its hinges,
>   so does a sluggard on his bed.
>   Proverbs 26:14 RSV

Am I a sluggard then? Is my disease making me a sinner? I find it hard to believe that a biological deficit in my brain could make me more of a sinner than I already am. But, depressed, I cannot even turn on my bed. I lie motionless, on my left side. It was on my left side that I was told to lie when I had preterm labor with both of my children. I hated lying still then; I felt caged. I was a human incubator, with no other function than to reach full term, which lay weeks and weeks ahead. But, depressed, I don't even mark the time. I sigh. I lie still, staring off into space, content to be caged within my brain. *Content?* No, such a word cannot be applied to a depressive. *Resigned.*

Accidie. Often translated as sloth. Is despair, as sloth, actually a sin? Is it actually like pride, murder, covetousness, lust, envy, gluttony, and anger? Of course there are sins that can come of the sin of despair. Maybe I am just too Protestant to speak about the deadly sins, but how can a physical disease be considered a sin? How can the fact of sloth caused by depression be considered in itself a sin? Yes, it may be a symptom of the power of sin, but to call it an individual sin is more than it can bear. The depressed may be slothful or may not be. The slothful may be depressed, but they are not necessarily so.

John Cassian (360–435) understood accidie to be a state of restlessness and inability to work or pray. According to Cassian, it affects monks and hermits who live mostly in seclusion. Of course, I always found seclusion to be poisonous to me when depressed. Assiduous prayer is prescribed by Cassian as the remedy for accidie.

Now, do I have accidie? Even though I am no monk, I suppose that I could be exhibiting accidie. But is accidie depression or some other form of mental illness? No, I would say clearly not. Many depressed people are slothful, yet this isn't the mark of depression for me or for my friends who are mothers. When you are a mother, you can never let go of your basic tasks except for very brief times. Intense pain while still engaging in the tasks of the day may be one of the mother's marks of depression. Most mothers, indeed, do not have the luxury of putting off the needs and desires of their children. If a mother is exceedingly ill, caretakers for the children will be necessary unless the husband is able not to work or the extended family can lend help. Postpartum depression can be very dangerous if no one is available to support the mother.

I have known very active people who were very depressed. While many depressed people may be slothful, the one who is slothful may just be self-indulgent. This is one of the keys to the stigma of mental illness: other people think that the mentally ill are just being self-indulgent. This may be true, but it is usually not true of people who are truly mentally ill.

Every time we can check despair and by the grace of God push it away and keep it from entering into our actions, God is glorified. But we must learn why it is that we feel whatever it is we are feeling. Feelings do matter; they just don't define us in our lives before God. Trying to understand our feelings is hard work and may take a long time. Patience, discipline, and endurance may be required. We must push the despair away and keep it from entering our actions insofar as we are able, while keeping the despair in mind enough to acknowledge it and maybe even to understand it. This is painful, it is not easy, but it may be a part of what God requires in this testing. And someday God may use us to help others facing a similar test.

Ultimately, though, I think the despair of any illness per se has no meaning. If it did, that meaning would be of God, because all meaning is of God. Any coherence in the midst of chaos, any sense in the midst of nonsense, is the work of God. If the despair had meaning, if there were in fact a purpose or reason for it, it would not be despair but something else. Mental illness is the lack of meaning, just as evil is the lack or privation of the good.

This is again one of the places where the theologian and the psychotherapist may part. I cannot say: *This* is the only reason I feel this way—this psychological scar, that chemical deficiency, this trauma, that breakdown in the personality. These may be good explanations on the biopsychosocial level, but they do not point to any ultimate meaning, any theological reality. Insofar as despair has a theological reality, it is evil. It is an absence of the good, an absence so present you can feel it, taste it, sometimes even, heaven forbid, see it and hear it. It is a black hole, a void, an emptiness that sucks into itself the sufferer. But we need to remember that God is the One who called order out of chaos, and who called the land into being as a boundary to the waters of death. And God calls even us into creation out of nothingness into life before him.

> "Woman, why are you weeping?" She said to them, "They have taken away my Lord, and I do not know where they have laid him."
>
> John 20:13

I thought I knew who Jesus was. I thought I could sense his presence. But in the symptoms of mental illness, I weep like Mary, "They have taken away my Lord, and I do not know where they have laid him." My fondest understandings about the love of the Lord have been turned inside out. My brain, my cognition, my memory, can't find Jesus. At least my soul itself is safe in the Lord, even if without my awareness.

Sin, suffering, and despair are thus linked in mental illness, yet not in a straightforward, one-to-one correspondence. People with mental illnesses, just like anyone else, may be suffering on account of the power of sin in the world; indeed, all suffering can be seen in this way. When I was sick, I needed to see God's presence even in this way, even in my suffering, even *because of* the power of sin. If I hadn't seen God in this way, as punishing my sin, as eradicating the force of sin in the world, then my suspicions would have been confirmed: that darkness was in fact my only companion and that God had indeed abandoned me.

10

Dark Night, Discipline, and the Hiddenness of God

> Darkness is not dark to you;
> the night is as bright as the day;
> darkness and light to you are both alike.
>
> Psalm 139:11 [139:12]

What is the dark night of the soul? How does it differ from mental illness, if at all? St. John of the Cross, Spanish mystic and theologian (1542–91), explains how the dark night of the soul is indeed different from depression. In a depression, "a lukewarm person is very lax and remiss in his will and spirit, and has no solicitude about serving God." On the other hand, in the dark night, the "person suffering the purgative dryness [dark night] is ordinarily solicitous, concerned and pained about not serving God."[1] In order for the soul to be filled by God, it must be emptied through the dark night and be purged by spiritual experience that, for John of the Cross, was harsh in its demands on the self. While his spirituality may seem severe, John was a man of deep charity and faith, and he wrote beautiful spiritual poetry.

The difference between the dark night and regular depression is that even in such a dark night the soul regrets its accidie. It has remorse for its lack of service to God. Should I be happy that at the very least I am pained about not serving God? At least I can claim the dark night of the soul instead of plain vanilla depression. The dark night of the soul can in fact be seen as the mirror image of depression: "Every experience in the one is contained in the other, but everything is reversed."[2]

But is John of the Cross right? Can it really be true that when depression passes, all is restored, but when the dark night passes, all is transformed? How can anyone live through depression, come out the other end, and not be transformed at least to some extent? I think that people who are engaged in psychotherapy, if they work hard with the right therapist, cannot help but come out the other end of depression changed. But I suppose John of the Cross would respond that the transformation of the soul is what we seek in the Christian life, not merely transformation of the personality. Of course John would know nothing of the assumptions of modern psychotherapy and would not have made such a distinction between personality and soul. But I can, since such concepts are at my fingertips. The transformation that happens in the dark night of the soul may be different from the personal transformation that happens in psychotherapy. The dark night of the soul actually enables one to love God more. Mental illness and/ or therapy may also make one love God more. But the dark night transforms the soul through hardships, which, as John's hardships did, can bring great blessings from God. In the end, for what it is worth, I do believe that I have had the soul's dark nights. And yet I do not deny that I have bipolar disorder.

Is it possible that God gives us the dark night as a test, to transform us? According to John this is so. We should allow ourselves to be transformed into God's likeness. But would God really lead us to conjure up all the methods possible of ending human life?

Would God create grotesque, life-denying, dangerous thoughts and visions? Would God so change our joy into mourning that we would want to return the gift of our own life to the Giver, like some unopened Christmas package from a spurned lover? I have a hard time believing all this. I think that these are not of God but of evil, that power which seeks to do harm to God's creatures, severing their relation to God.

Of course, to speak of the dark night of the soul is anathema to many in the psychiatric field. I was told by one of my psychiatrists years ago not to equate depression with any religious experience such as the dark night of the soul, nor to interpret my illness in religious terms. I never asked him why; I just assumed that he didn't want religious language to be mixed with medical language. I did try to tell him, however, that religious language covers all and every aspect of being, that I could not simply separate it from his profession's language and concepts. He looked disgusted.

Mental illness is a biological disease. It is the result of a series of events and chemical reactions in the brain. Medications and psychotherapy both can change the metabolic function of the brain. Yes, I agree, but so does prayer. And all can be transformed by the dark night.

Julian of Norwich (1342–1416), English mystic from an earlier period than John, says the following of the relation between sorrow and transformation: "Before miracles come sorrow, anguish and tribulation. [God] does not will that we be overly depressed by the sorrows and storms that come our way, because that has always been the condition before miracles come."

Do any miracles come from mental illness? I suppose that could depend on how we define a miracle. If we understand a miracle as did Augustine as that which causes us to marvel before the power and goodness of God, I can imagine that miracles could indeed result from mental illness. I certainly have known miracles of resurrection to come from my own illness. Not that I would wish mental illness on anyone who was hoping for a miracle—or on anyone who was not. But this does lead me to wonder how

we might use Julian's insight as she does, as a way of attempting
not to drown in our present sorrow. Psychotropic medication is
supposed to relieve the symptoms of the illness themselves. And
psychotherapy is supposed to help us understand ourselves, what
makes us ill and why. But based on Julian's insight, what should the
Christian do in addition to making use of these resources? Would
we need specifically to welcome the sorrow rather than seek relief
from it? No, I think Julian would say that sorrow in itself is not
to be sought, and relief *is* to be sought, and that from God. Of
course, she is the one who said, "All thing shall be well, and all
thing shall be well, and all manner of thing shall be well." Still,
the transformation that can come of sorrow is to be welcomed.

> To keep me from being too elated [by an abundance of revelations],
> a thorn was given me in the flesh, a messenger of Satan to torment
> me, to keep me from being too elated. Three times I appealed to
> the Lord about this, that it would leave me, but he said to me, "My
> grace is sufficient for you, for power is made perfect in weakness."
>
> 2 Corinthians 12:7–9

I do know that compassion is one of those lessons I must learn
from my illness. Doesn't everything boil down to that? God still has
much work to do to overcome my being *incurvata in me*, curved
in upon myself, the root of sin. I still have far to go. My struggle
with my thorn, my own weakness, is not finished, and I know it
will never be finished in this life. But I object. St. Paul speaks of his
thorn in the flesh, but we don't really know what he was talking
about. In any case, there Satan gave the thorn. And there, even
there, God did not allow it to be removed but intended to use it
for good. Can anything good really ever come of any illness, even
mental illness—a medical disease that can cripple the brain, mind,
and even body? "Take every thought captive to obey Christ" (2 Cor.
10:5). Could Paul have known of my condition, which itself is the
captor, which itself wrings my mind dry of thoughts of Christ
and wants to hand my soul over to hell?

Plenty of Christians before me must have had this difficulty, and many Christians surely will after me. Mental illness is not an indication of the weakness of one's faith. It may be, however, a test and should be met like all other tests: with prayer that God will see us through it faithfully, that we may be seen faithful, and that we should be found at the last without reproach, that God will use it to our benefit and us to his glory.

After all, as I have said, faith is not primarily a feeling. It is an act. Sometimes the most pleasing thing to God is our obedience and rendering of thanks even when we don't feel at all thankful. Jesus said that even the hypocrites love those who love them. They love when it is easy. But the most valuable thing in God's sight is loving the unlovely, loving when no return is expected, when one has no love, hoping when hope is not seen. Then we really have to admit that all our loves and all our hopes are ultimately borrowed from God anyway.

> Now the great thing is this: we are consecrated and dedicated to God in order that we may thereafter think, speak, meditate and do, nothing except to his glory. . . . We are not our own: let not our reason nor our will, therefore, sway our plans and deeds. We are not our own: let us therefore not set it as our goal to seek what is expedient for us according to the flesh. We are not our own: in so far as we can, let us therefore forget ourselves and all that is ours. Conversely, we are God's: let us therefore live for him and die for him. We are God's: let his wisdom and will therefore rule all our actions. We are God's: let all the parts of our life accordingly strive toward him as our only lawful goal.
>
> John Calvin (1509–64)
> (cf. Rom. 14:7–9; 1 Cor. 6:19–20)

From a theological perspective, the most dangerous thing about mental illness is that it can lock us in ourselves, convincing us that we are indeed our own, and completely on our own, isolated in our distress. Darkness *is* my only companion. Mental illness can

be to us a veil that shrouds our consecration to God, blocking out
the glory of the Holy One. Our wounds fester. Our remoteness
from the source of our healing increases. Mental illness shuts all
windows and doors to the soul so that we cannot speak, meditate, or do anything to the glory of God, or so it seems. All is
experienced as pain. We are locked in ourselves, unable to forget
our pain. How does the Christian endure such remoteness from
the source of life?

> O Lord, calm the waves of this heart; calm its tempests. Calm your-
> self, O my soul, so that the divine can act in you. Calm yourself,
> O my soul, so that God is able to repose in you, so that his peace
> may cover you. Yes, Father in heaven, often have we found that the
> world cannot give us peace, O but make us feel that you are able to
> give peace; let us know the truth of your promise: that the whole
> world may not be able to take away your peace.
>
> Søren Kierkegaard (1813–55)

I must value myself, and not disvalue myself, such as would im-
poverish my Creator. But if I try to talk this way to my psychiatrist,
he may be convinced that I do not value myself at all, that I have
to look to the divine "projection" of myself in order to validate
myself, give myself reason to be. Here is another place where the
chasm between the religious patient and the nonreligious therapist
simply cannot be bridged. Is he right? Am I really not valuing myself for myself? Yes, he is right. But the value I place on his being
right is the opposite of that which he claims it should be. I do
not value myself for myself, but this in itself does not necessarily
indicate illness on my part, spiritually or mentally. I value myself
for the One who created and redeemed me and who will raise me
on the last day. This is the only true self-affirmation, the only one
that makes any sense within biblical and orthodox Christianity.
Bernard of Clairvaux (1090–1153), following Augustine, says that
the highest form of spiritual achievement is learning to love the
self for the sake of God.

But one of my psychiatrists can't get it, won't get it. He looked at me as if I were some animal from the zoo, as if I had been irredeemably hoodwinked by false consciousness. Without the triune God (as though there were really some "without" where I could stand), I bear only ephemeral value. This is not bad. This is simply true. And by the grace of God, I have been engrafted into Christ's identity in my baptism. So this truth is not bad news but good news. Incredibly good news. Mental illness veils this news, masks this news. How can a secular psychiatrist help me here? Only in spite of himself, I suppose. Only by the grace of the very God he despises. But I can't give up on the possibility that he could help me. A friend pointed out to me that if God could use a talking ass to guide Balaam, then a secular psychiatrist can help us. After all, the angel Gabriel said to Mary, "Nothing will be impossible with God" (Luke 1:37), when he announced that she would bear the Christ without having yet "known a man." And as the angel said to Abraham upon hearing Sarah laugh at the promise of a son, "Is anything too hard for the LORD?" (Gen. 18:14 RSV). Our faith is full of surprises. I just can't stand the illness that veils them from me.

> He has not dealt with us according to our sins,
>   nor rewarded us according to our wickedness.
> For as the heavens are high above the earth,
>   so is his mercy great upon those who fear him.
> As far as the east is from the west,
>   so far has he removed our sins from us.
> As a father cares for his children,
>   so does the LORD care for those who fear him.
> For he himself knows whereof we are made;
>   he remembers that we are but dust.
>
> Psalm 103:10–14

Why is this illness happening? I never ask "Why me?" Only "Why this?" I accept God's sovereignty to afflict and to comfort whom he wills, but why this kind of affliction? How can I do your work, God, in this state? Do the dead praise you from the grave?

> "My child, do not regard lightly the discipline of the Lord,
>   or lose heart when you are punished by him;
> for the Lord disciplines those whom he loves,
>   and chastises every child whom he accepts."

Endure trials for the sake of discipline. God is treating you as children.

Hebrews 12:5–7, quoting Proverbs 3:11–12

Are you disciplining me with madness? Can that really be? I will try to understand this, because this pain seems so near to the demonic that I find it hard to understand the discipline of the Merciful One in it. But I will try to understand. As Hebrews said earlier, I have not yet resisted the powers of evil to the point of shedding my blood, to the point of martyrdom for the name of Jesus. I suppose I should be grateful that my battle is internal and is not against those who could destroy my body in order to quench the hope of my soul. But my body does not need to be destroyed to quench my hope, because inside of me the battle rages against that very hope, to convince me that that hope is mere illusion, that pain is all there is. And the interior battle that strives to quench my hope threatens to destroy my very body. But not in the name of Jesus—against the name of Jesus, in hatred of the name of Jesus. My God, my God, why have you abandoned me?

> Now, discipline always seems painful rather than pleasant at the time, but later it yields the peaceful fruit of righteousness to those who have been trained by it.
>   Therefore lift your drooping hands and strengthen your weak knees, and make straight paths for your feet, so that what is lame may not be put out of joint, but rather be healed.

Hebrews 12:11–13

Be healed. Lift your drooping hands. Strengthen your weak knees. How can I do that? My hands do nothing but droop. My knees are nothing but weak. "There is no health in my flesh" (Ps. 38:3).

How can I be healed? You speak to me in Hebrews as though I can do it myself, as though I have the power to "snap out of this." I seriously doubt this. I have tried, and tried, and will not stop trying even though I desperately want to stop trying. Make straight my paths, you say. I am lame and cannot walk twisted paths. When I sprained my ankle, I literally could not walk except on the most level of surfaces without pain. What then are straight paths for the sprained brain? Even when you suggest that I see this as discipline (for surely Christians read these ancient texts as speaking directly to us even now), you are not suggesting that I impale myself on the discipline. You tell me to take courage and make sure that I take the straight paths, the way of righteousness that will not hurt my already sprained brain but will help to put the lame places in me right.

> My brothers and sisters, whenever you face trials of any kind, consider it nothing but joy, because you know that the testing of your faith produces endurance; and let endurance have its full effect, so that you may be mature and complete, lacking in nothing.
>
> James 1:2–4

Consider it nothing but joy. My brain disorder itself is supposed to cause me joy? Not because the Christian is meant to flagellate herself, or because we are to look for troubles and tests in life, but that trials may be considered cause for joy since they produce endurance and maturity. I wonder what my psychiatrist would think about this.

> My child, do not despise the LORD's discipline
>   or be weary of his reproof,
> for the LORD reproves the one he loves,
>   as a father the son in whom he delights.
>   Proverbs 3:11–12

Is God really treating me as a child? Surely then it must be like Isaac in Genesis 22, the chosen, the child of the promise, whom

God tells Abraham to sacrifice on Mount Moriah. That is the child I am. Not a dear child, not one whom God protects. Yet Isaac was indeed the child of the promise: "Take your son, your only son Isaac, whom you love . . ." (Gen. 22:2). And at the last moment God told Abraham not to slay him. Is this what it means to endure all trials for the sake of discipline? Again, my doctors and therapists would cough, objecting. But still I am told that we are to endure all trials for the sake of discipline. Truly you are a God who hides himself (Isa. 45:15).

Isaiah's statement that God hides himself is taken up in the history of Christian theology. Martin Luther (1483–1546), the great Reformer, among others, believed that we know God best *sub contrario*, or in his hiddenness. Blaise Pascal (1623–62), too, worked with this theme of the hiddenness of God in his *Pensées*. For Pascal, "what can be seen on earth points to neither the total absence nor the obvious presence of divinity, but to the presence of a hidden God" (*Pensées* 449). This is because for Pascal, and arguably for Isaiah as well, the existence of God is not obvious to human reason. If God were not hidden in some sense, humanity would not be required to seek assistance in the knowledge of God. This would result in our own hubris and further cut us off from God's presence. In this sense, the hiddenness of God is revelatory.

But when I say that God is a God that hides himself, is this what I mean? Is human arrogance the problem? Is human reason the problem? Is revelation the problem? No, here suffering is the problem. God hides himself from my suffering, in my suffering. My question is this: *How long, O Lord? How long?*

> God, give us grace to accept with serenity the things that cannot be changed, courage to change the things that should be changed, and the wisdom to distinguish the one from the other.
>
> Reinhold Niebuhr (1892–1971)[3]

I cannot change my health, or lack of it. I have a brain disorder from which I will never "recover." There is no "cure." There may be someday. Researchers are experimenting with magnets and electronic implants. But these are not yet readily available. My doctors and I have, however, finally found a constellation of medications that provide me relief from the deepest and longest depressions, from the randomness of hypomania, from the indignity of hearing and seeing things others do not. At this point, I only occasionally have my days when the world is so bleak that I am dismantled. I usually spend such days either in agony, still functioning as I must with the children and my responsibilities at church, or by retreating into bed and merciful, forgetful sleep. Will I spend my entire life in such blithering antipodes between elation and productivity, or despair and sleep? At least I can sleep. Some people have the curse of not even being able to sleep, nerves rough hewn from insomnia. *God, give us grace to accept with serenity the things that cannot be changed.*

> I waited patiently upon the LORD,
>   he stooped to me and heard my cry.
> He lifted me out of the desolate pit, out of the mire and clay;
>   he set my feet upon a high cliff and made my footing
>   sure.
> He put a new song in my mouth,
> a song of praise to our God;
>   many shall see, and stand in awe,
>   and put their trust in the LORD. . . .
> Though I am poor and afflicted,
>   the Lord will have regard for me.
> You are my helper and my deliverer;
>   do not tarry, O my God.
>   Psalm 40:1–3, 18–19 [17]

Like Israel brought back from exile, I have been bought with a price. "You are not your own, you are the Lord's." A fountain in an arid land is the Holy Spirit to my soul. If only I could remember when mentally ill that this is true. Maybe this is my vocation in life, praising God even in the midst of humiliation and sheer hatred of self. Or rather hatred of my condition, but it feels like hatred of self. I plead for compassion for self, for gentleness toward self, but it seems illusory.

> Grant, I beg you, merciful Lord, that the designs of a new and better life, which by your grace I have now formed, may not pass away without effect. Incite and enable me, by your Holy Spirit, to improve the time which you shall grant me; to avoid all evil thoughts, words, and actions; and to do all the duties which you shall set before me. Hear my prayer, O Lord, for the sake of Jesus Christ.
>
> Samuel Johnson (1702–84)

To improve the time which you shall grant me . . . Gracious and Holy One, give me your mercy to avoid the thoughts in the blackness which separate me from you, which lead only to death. I have no strength of my own to avoid them, to steer around them; my ship is tossed and cast about by the Powers Grim. Please, dear God, have mercy on me, that I may not do that which would permanently separate me from my family, for the well-being of my family and to the glory of your name.

> With weeping they shall come,
>   and with consolations I will lead them back,
> I will let them walk by brooks of water,
>   in a straight path in which they shall not stumble;
> for I have become a father to Israel.
>
> Jeremiah 31:9

In such prophecies of redemption I find peace. I find hope. I find comfort. Sometimes all I can do is read Scripture and the prayers of the faithful, such as these, just to keep going.

> Blessed be the God and Father of our Lord Jesus Christ, the Father of mercies and the God of all consolation, who consoles us in all our affliction, so that we may be able to console those who are in any affliction with the consolation with which we ourselves are

consoled by God. For just as the sufferings of Christ are abundant for us, so also our consolation is abundant through Christ.

                                        2 Corinthians 1:3–5

This reminds me of God's comfort, of God's tender care, without which I am lost, adrift in my illness. It reminds me of the consolation not only of Christ but also of discipleship. In our discipleship and care of others, we learn of the sufferings of Christ and therefore of his care. And this in turn means that we can know and serve the experience of those who also go through adversity and suffering.

These passages give me great comfort. Where is the God of anger, of punishment of sin, the hidden God? Not here.

> O Lord, reassure me with your quickening Spirit; without you I can do nothing. Mortify in me all ambition, vanity, vainglory, worldliness, pride, selfishness and resistance to God, and fill me with love, peace, and all the fruits of the Spirit. O Lord, I know not what I am, but to you I flee for refuge. I would surrender myself to you, trusting your precious promises and against hope believing in hope. You are the same yesterday, today, and for ever; and therefore, waiting on the Lord, I trust I shall at length renew my strength.
>
> William Wilberforce (1759–1833)

Mortify in me all ambition. I cannot work as I would. I am unreliable, my worst fear and disillusionment. I have had to back out of speaking engagements again this year. This decision was exquisitely difficult for me. Difficult because of my self-image, and exquisite because as I made the decisions to back out, I breathed a prayer of mercy and thanks at the relief. My self-image is of a strong woman, capable of taking on and taking on and taking on. I can no longer be this woman. Maybe I never really was. I must now be more realistic, relying on the power of the Holy Spirit to "mortify in me all vanity, vainglory, worldliness, pride, selfishness and resistance to God." To fall into God's hands is a wondrous thing.

I lift up my eyes to the hills;
    from where is my help to come?
My help comes from the LORD,
    the maker of heaven and earth.
He will not let your foot be moved,
    and he who watches over you will not fall asleep.
Behold, he who keeps watch over Israel
    shall neither slumber nor sleep;
The LORD himself watches over you;
    the LORD is your shade at your right hand,
So that the sun shall not strike you by day,
    nor the moon by night.
The LORD shall preserve you from all evil;
    it is he who shall keep you safe.
The LORD shall watch over your going out and your com-
    ing in,
    from this time forth for evermore.

                                       Psalm 121

I once asked a rabbi I knew if he believed this, that the One who watches over Israel shall neither slumber nor sleep. I am sure that some rabbis do believe this, but this one answered that he did not and could not believe it. If God watched over Israel, how could the Holocaust have happened? Now—not to trivialize that horrendous event of history—I have had my own burnt offering to the Lord. How can I believe that God does not sleep through my pain? Does the Lord really watch our going out and coming in? I have to answer yes. I must answer positively because Scripture witnesses that indeed God does not sleep, does watch, does preserve us. The question then is how, why, when does he watch? But not if or whether he watches.

    You who fear the Lord, wait for his mercy;
        and turn not aside, lest you fall.
    You who fear the Lord, trust in him,
        and your reward will not fail;
    You who fear the Lord, hope for good things,
        for everlasting joy and mercy.

                                Sirach 2:7–9 RSV

Hope. When we are in a state of severe mental illness, hope is far from us. This is why we need the scriptures and the community of faith. They contribute faith and hope to us as from a well we cannot now reach. We do see that the well is there. We must grab on to the hope of the community which is objectively there whether we can feel it or not, see it or not.

> Take off the garment of your sorrow and affliction,
>   O Jerusalem,
>   and put on for ever the beauty of the glory from God.
> Put on the robe of righteousness from God;
>   put on your head the diadem of the glory of the
>   Everlasting.
>
> Baruch 5:1–2 RSV

Slowly I am taking off the garment of my sorrow and affliction, because of medication, a caring therapist, an excellent psychiatrist, a loving and patient husband, two children, friends and family who love me, and lots of prayer. Despite my frequent desires, I will not leave my family by harming myself irreparably. Taking off the garment of sorrow and affliction here in Baruch appears to be something that Jerusalem is doing herself, something she is commanded to do on her own. I must do this actively, on my own. I must fight the depressions with every ounce of courage and strength. *Put on for ever the beauty of the glory from God.*

> Why do you say, O Jacob,
>   and speak, O Israel,
> "My way is hidden from the LORD,
>   and my right is disregarded by my God"?
> Have you not known? Have you not heard?
> The LORD is the everlasting God,
>   the Creator of the ends of the earth.
> He does not faint or grow weary;
>   his understanding is unsearchable.
> He gives power to the faint,
>   and strengthens the powerless.

Even youths will faint and be weary,
   and the young will fall exhausted;
but they who wait upon the LORD shall renew their strength,
   they shall mount up with wings like eagles,
they shall run and not be weary,
   they shall walk and not faint.

Isaiah 40:27–31

Strength is not even necessarily to the young, nor health to the youthful, but those who serve the LORD will glorify the LORD in waiting upon him. Teach me, LORD, to wait. My health is in waiting upon you, serving you, praising you all my days.

Because God did not make death,
   he does not delight in the death of the living.

Wisdom of Solomon 1:13

I cannot believe that God wills death or sickness. In the garden of Eden, the first pair was warned, "In the day that you eat of [the fruit of the tree of the knowledge of good and of evil] you shall die" (Gen. 2:17). Their death is not God's will. God sets his commandment over them, and they break it. Only with their reaching out and eating of the tree do they become subject to evil and death, but with God's forewarning.

So I cannot believe that God wills my necrotizing brain to kill me, even when I am convinced that death would be the least painful exit. *God does not delight in the death of the living.*

You will forget your misery;
   you will remember it as waters that have passed away.
And your life will be brighter than the noonday;
   its darkness will be like the morning.
And you will have confidence, because there is hope;
   you will be protected and take your rest in safety.
You will lie down, and no one will make you afraid;
   many will entreat your favor.

Job 11:16–19

Just as it was the memories of Israel and the church that buoyed me during my illness, so now I need to forget: to forget my misery, to remember it as waters that have passed away. My life will indeed be brighter than the noonday; I will be protected and take my rest in safety. Just as before I needed to remember the mercies of God in the past, now I must forget the suffering and evil of my illness, in order to let God heal and protect me.

> Even though you [my brothers and enemies] intended to do me harm, God intended it for good.
>
> Genesis 50:20

Can I really say that God intended it for good—this pain, this wretchedness, this humiliation? If all of God's intentions for us are good, why do we suffer? Luther said we suffer because of the grace of God. I have a hard time believing this. I think we suffer because of evil, the deprivation of the good, but even still God can work his grace out of our suffering.

> Batter my heart, three person'd God; for you
> As yet but knock, breathe, shine, and seek to mend;
> That I may rise, and stand, o'erthrow me, and bend
> Your force to break, blow, burn, and make me new.
>
> John Donne (1572–1631)

Take up your battering ram, loving Lord, and splinter the gates of my heart. Do not knock gently. Behold, I stand at the door and I wait for your knocking. Please, dear God, there is nothing I desire more, for nothing else will lead to my health but your force. Make me new. Make me new. Renew me.

11

Health and Prayer

I waited patiently upon the LORD;
    he stooped to me and heard my cry.
He lifted me out of the desolate pit, out of the mire
        and clay;
    he set my feet upon a high cliff and made my
        footing sure.

Psalm 40:1–2

Be not afraid to pray—
to pray is right.
Pray, if thou canst, with hope;
But ever pray,
Though hope be weak
or sick with long delay;
Pray in the darkness,
if there be no light.

Hartley Coleridge,
1796–1849

Pray? Pray? Are you kidding? My mind is mush, jello, the leavings
at the bottom of the garbage can. How can I pray? I don't even
want to. I am steamed, furious, sputtering angry. Pray with hope,
my foot. Pray in the darkness? Well, that would be the only place
I could pray, because there is no light, but even there I can't pray,
not now and apparently never again. I will never get better. I am
simply going progressively mad. Tick by tock by tick, with each
turn of the clock's gears I am closer to insanity. And you tell me to
pray. I am just glad you prayed, Hartley Coleridge, you, Hebrews,
you, King David, because I can't. I will pray your prayers, lean on
your faith. I have none of my own.

> Ah, Lord, my prayers are dead, my affections dead, and
>   my heart is dead.
> But thou art a living God and I bear myself upon thee.
>   William Bridge (1600–1670)

I was cleaning up the garden to try to keep myself busy, to try
to keep the pain of the latest depression at bay. Busyness is an
important part of healing for me, or at least of staving off the
symptoms of depressive disorder. I had been piling the daylily
leaves, long, golden-brown, and spent, on the grass by the garage
as I pulled more. I went to the pile to throw down another armful
and noticed that the scrolling leaves spelled "Jesus." I blinked,
glanced back, and the letters spelling out my Lord's name were
gone, receded into the pile of so many leaves.

I am supposed to be getting better. Why is this still happening?
Then I realized that the word I saw was not like the severed fingers
of my daughter, nor like the highway rolling up in smoke. This
was a good vision, a nonthreatening vision, a comforting vision.
I asked myself why I would be seeing that word, *Jesus*, and not
another. An old hymn immediately came to my mind.

> What a friend we have in Jesus,
> All our sins and griefs to bear,

> We must never be discouraged,
> Take it to the Lord in prayer.
> Do thy friends despise, forsake thee?
> Is there trouble ev'rywhere?
> Jesus knows our every weakness,
> Thou wilt find a solace there.
> Joseph M. Scriven (1820–86)

And it consoled me. Actually consoled me. *Thou wilt find a solace there.* Jesus can heal the soul even while using the sickness of the brain. Darkness is not my only companion. *What a friend we have in Jesus.* The kind who won't leave us. Why did it take me so long to remember this?

I had not been praying for my own healing at this point. I certainly do not mean to generalize and say that all mentally ill people should follow me in this. But the only prayer I could muster was for strength to endure this. There were of course times when the shadow of an inkling crossed my mind to pray for healing, but for some reason it did not seem the right thing to do. How strange. It just didn't fit. Almost as if it were blasphemous to pray for healing, to be rid of despair, to be freed of the horror of bouncing from high to low. I am not called to pray for healing from this, only for strength to endure. This is because I believe that God still has much to teach me through this, and that some of what he will teach I can't even yet begin to imagine.

> For surely I know the plans I have for you, says the LORD, plans for your welfare and not for harm, to give you a future with hope. Then when you call upon me and come and pray to me, I will hear you. When you search for me, you will find me; if you seek me with all your heart, I will let you find me, says the LORD, and I will restore your fortunes and gather you from all the nations and all the places where I have driven you, says the LORD, and I will bring you back to the place from which I sent you into exile.
>
> Jeremiah 29:11–14

But now I can pray. God has let me find him. Health begins to shine through the pain. It feels like water on parched lips, like salve on a wound. I cannot believe how sick I was, how beginning to be "normal" feels so amazing.

What was the worth of being sick? While before I felt like a mouse being batted about by a huge cat, now I feel healing. And I feel that God is the ultimate source of that healing, even though medications and therapy are part of it. What was God's relation to my suffering? In what sense did he cause or allow my suffering, and to what end? This is a central question for the Christian who suffers from mental illness or any other agonizing affliction: What is God's relationship to my pain?

It seems to me that the answer is that God is present throughout, even when it doesn't feel like it. It also can feel as if God is the author of the pain, because so much learning goes on throughout and in the suffering. But how can I say that God causes suffering? Maybe, as with Job, God allows the suffering as a test. I have indeed been tested as by fire.

What then is the relationship between the sufferings of Christ and the Christian sufferer? "I am now rejoicing in my sufferings for your sake, and in my flesh I am completing what is lacking in Christ's affliction for the sake of his body, that is, the church" (Col. 1:24). The writer of Colossians sees a clear relationship between his own sufferings and the sufferings of Christ. His own sufferings work to the health of the body of Christ. This is cause for rejoicing. After all, how can one complete what is lacking in Christ's affliction except with rejoicing? I do not easily rejoice in my sufferings per se, but here if I follow the apostle, I must rejoice, insofar as my sufferings are mini-reflections of the redeeming suffering of Christ. They redound to the benefit of the body. And I do hope that this is true. But if I were to keep quiet about my sufferings, this would not be true. They might be a benefit to me, but not to those around me.

Those who are healthy, who have never been sick, will not know the joy and release and comfort God gives us in health. You have to know lack of health in order to rejoice in good health. You have to know what it is like to be, or at least feel, cut off from the body in order to enjoy its community. Not necessarily mentally ill, of course, but truly ill, sick unto death.

> Comfort, O comfort my people,
>   says your God.
> Speak tenderly to Jerusalem,
>   and cry to her
> that she has served her term,
>   that her penalty is paid,
> that she has received from the LORD's hand
>   double for all her sins.
>   Isaiah 40:1–2

Comfort here was for the people as a whole, for a nation whose warfare will be over and whose sin forgiven. To read this Scripture as addressed to me, in the singular, is not to make a category error; truly Scripture speaks in more ways than just straightforward ones, even while our understanding is based on a plain reading. Nothing violates the Scripture here for me to take this comfort on myself, to claim it as my own, now in the twenty-first century. I read this passage as comfort to me, not only to Israel, not only to the present Israel of God, the church of Jews and gentiles.

How do I understand my sufferings in relation to God, except through prayer? Prayer has been for me a large comfort, both my own prayers and the prayers of others on my behalf. However, those prayers on my behalf were fewer than they could have been, since I did not tell many people what was wrong. This is part of the tragedy of the stigma of mental illness for the Christian. There was one friend, though, who prayed for me faithfully and constantly for years, to whom I will always be grateful. And, of course, my family and a few other friends who also knew of my illness supported me in prayer.

Some studies of the efficacy of prayer have led even the scientific world to admit that prayer may contribute something important to the healing of body, mind, and soul. For example, Harvard researchers surveyed more than two thousand adults, finding that prayer helped in more cases than did visits to the doctor for depression, anxiety disorders, arthritis, back pain, and cancer. A well-known experiment by cardiologist Randolph Boyd likewise showed the importance of prayer in healing. In this double-blind, randomized experiment, some cardiology patients were prayed for and some were not. Patients, nurses, and doctors did not know which patients were in which group. The results showed that the prayed-for patients had a markedly lesser need for antibiotics, they were less likely to develop pulmonary edema, and none of them needed intubation.[1] Of course, the Christian faith does not depend on such studies to value prayer.

I have always been very wary of "faith healers." Liberal Christianity has been an influence on me since my youth in this regard, and it tends to shy away from the idea that prayer would be objectively effective except insofar as it changes the one who prays. Faith healers made me think of hucksters. Not all healers are alike, however, and not all are hucksters. We once invited a healing priest who worked in our Diocese to our parish for a healing workshop. I think this was before I was priested. He stressed that the prayers would begin the healing process but that healing would rarely be a dramatic event. The workshop involved among other things gathering the congregation around one person at a time and praying with the laying on of hands. At one point, I was called to sit in the designated chair at the center of the congregation. They put their hands on me, and those on the perimeter of the circle who couldn't reach me laid their hands on those in front of them. They began to pray. I do not remember the specific words the priest used, but I was overwhelmed. In part it was that all those people were around me, praying for me, and I felt a deep gratitude and tenderness. In part it was that I felt all those years of blackness being sucked out of me. I wept. I don't know how long this lasted. Maybe ten minutes or longer. All I know is that since then I have been doing consistently better and better, despite my prior suspicions of this type of healing.

Now, I would never use this experience as an excuse to stop seeing my therapist or to cut off medication. Even though at times I have certainly wanted to do this, this desire has come from a perverse need for independence rather than the confidence that I had begun the process of being healed by prayer.

In addition, I would never want to suggest by relating this experience that prayer is a tool to be used at one's whim for the betterment of life. Of course it is indeed for the betterment of life, and of course it is one of the "spiritual tools" that the Christian relies upon, but it is never to be understood in an instrumental sense. In prayer we are not to "heap up empty phrases" like the hypocrites as though to twist God's arm into action as if one could do that anyhow (Matt. 6:7). This is blasphemy. But for the Christian, prayer is our relationship with God, and it is proper that we make our requests known to God. It is appropriate to hope and to ask for healing, but it is not theologically appropriate to assume or to hope for a moment that we can manipulate the power of God in our prayers. Even so, God tells us to let our requests be made known. And Jesus approves of the woman in the parable who kept annoying the judge until he vindicated her against her adversary (Luke 18:5).

Since prayer is key to the Christian's relationship with God, it will naturally bring health in God's good time. To be brought into relationship with the living God, to be able to touch the fringe of Jesus's prayer shawl, bears to us God's curative power. Ultimately, healing may be on the other side of illness, through the path of the dark night, and past difficult experiences. But to know God is to know eternal life. Prayer will bring health—even for the bent and broken mind of the mentally ill.

PART THREE

Living with
Mental Illness

12

How Clergy, Friends, and Family Can Help

He will feed his flock like a shepherd;
    he will gather the lambs in his arms,
and carry them in his bosom,
    and gently lead the mother sheep.

Isaiah 40:11

I was visited by two clergy members, both friends, during one of my stays in the hospital. They came and stayed, and stayed. I think they thought I must have been bored and needed entertaining. But in fact I was bone-tired. I just gave my tight, skin-stretching smile and nodded while they chatted away.

I think people in general don't know how to treat those whose mental health is not as good as their own. They are often nervous and too uncomfortable to understand that the mental hospital is a respite for the patient and that visitation should be kept short. I suggest no more than ten or fifteen minutes. This probably goes for the physically ill as well. While people may think that the hospital is a boring place and that the patient needs conversation and entertainment, in fact hospitals can be exhausting. Nurses and roommates, not to mention side effects of new medications, can interrupt sleep. For the psychiatric patient, simply being in the presence of a friend or loved one can be a trial.

The visitor should always inquire after the health of the patient. Don't start complaining about your own problems or even someone else's just to have something to talk about. Follow the patient's lead. If she wants to talk about meaningful things such as her fears and worries, then make observations. Gently inquire. But don't pry. Remember that for the mentally ill person, especially when hospitalized, conversation can be an uphill battle.

Offer to read Scripture. Invite the patient to indicate her own requests, but do not press here either. Making decisions is often difficult for patients. Psalm 139 was and remains a comfort to me. Offer to pray. If you have an oil stock, offer anointing. If you have a Communion kit, offer Communion. But that should be about all. Be out of there in fifteen minutes to leave the patient to recover, unless she requests a longer visit. Offer to come more than once. Don't abandon her in the hospital.

How can clergy help a parishioner with a mental illness before hospitalization has become necessary? This is tricky, because clergy are not necessarily trained to recognize symptoms. The signs may be subtle. Here it will be important for clergy to know their flock: personalities, family situations, challenges they face. Personal distance from the flock will not be helpful either to the conscientious pastor or to her congregation. Do you notice anyone consistently tearing up during the hymns or prayers? Are you aware of any familial problems or causes for grief? Has anyone become unexpectedly less communicative, smiling less frequently, gaining or losing weight? Unusually timid, reserved, even angry? The biggest mistake here is for the priest or pastor to take this kind of behavior personally. Do you notice a usually competent and capable parishioner having difficulties with others, talking to herself, looking confused, making non sequiturs, dressing in an uncharacteristic manner? You may have spotted symptoms. The question is now: what to do?

What I personally have done is simply to drop the person an email, which is less personal and therefore possibly less threatening than a phone call or face-to-face communication. This may mean that the parishioner will feel more at ease to express her feelings. Then I might invite the person out for coffee or lunch. It is, after all, an important part of pastoral care to inquire about the state of a parishioner's soul and mind, in part to keep in touch, in part to know what to pray for. During face-to-face communication, however, do not push and prod. Allow the person time to talk. Be warm, open, but not chatty. If you suspect depression, ask the parishioner openly about this; she may have already sought out the help of a therapist. (I think it is a good idea for all clergy to keep an updated list of therapists and psychiatrists whom they have vetted in advance.) Keep in touch with the parishioner, pray for her, and let her know you are praying for her.

Signs to look for when dealing with mania are odd behaviors, such as changed forms of speech, sometimes pressured or excessive. Look for changes in dress, such as excessively flamboyant clothing on someone who normally might not dress that way. Look for overflowing ideas, evidence of excessive spending, or hypersexuality. Look for aggressiveness, enormous energy, or paranoia. Mania may be easier to spot than depression or hypomania; its symptoms are outward, while depression's symptoms are more inward. A person in a hypomanic state may just seem like someone having a good time, being the life of the party.

What if you are dealing with a case of potential suicide attempt or possible danger to others? This is trickier still. Some of the signs of suicidality to watch for are self-isolation; morbid talk of death, either about one's own or another's; expression of despair; the giving away of prized possessions; self-harm such as burn or razor tracks on the arms; and, especially, admission of wanting to hurt oneself or others. Don't be afraid to ask if the person is having thoughts of this nature. Hopefully the parishioner will be open with you. You will not "push" her to suicide by asking pointed questions. Just do so with care and concern. In fact, asking if she is thinking of hurting herself may not be pointed enough. Ask: are you thinking of ending your life? This is one of the most important points in suicide prevention: talk openly, calmly, frankly, in a nonjudgmental tone. This is not a time to be shy or awkward. A pastoral caregiver who doesn't want to "overreact" is putting everyone in physical, emotional, and spiritual danger. Don't fool yourself into thinking you can handle such a situation on your own. Major Mental Illnesses are not for the pastor or priest to diagnose or treat unless he or she is also a medical doctor. Professional psychiatric help should be sought immediately. At the same time, the psychiatrist is not trained to evaluate the potential religious content or import of psychiatric symptoms.

I used to think that confidentiality meant absolute silence on everything. Having seen too much illness turn to tragedy, I no longer understand even taking confessions in that way. I have struggled with this over the years, but now I have come to believe that confidences should be broken if there is compelling evidence that someone is in danger to self or others. If the confidence must be broken, any information disclosed is to be used only with great discretion. The pastoral caregiver must always maintain the parishioner's privacy whenever possible. At this point, simply call 911. Do not feel guilty for intervening in this way. How would you feel if you were not to call and, God forbid, your parishioner were to kill herself or someone else? In some states, when such a 911 call is made, the police and the ambulance will both come to the scene. This may be frightening both for you (*Did I do the right thing?*) and for your parishioner (*Why are the police coming after me?*). If the patient is in a manic or psychotic state, be prepared for a scuffle. The police are there to manage an uncontrollable patient, but sadly they are not always trained well in respecting the dignity of all people, especially those with mental illnesses.

Your parishioner may want you to go with her in the ambulance (depending on the EMT's permission). Or she may want you to meet the ambulance at the hospital. If you are willing and able to offer this, it may be a comfort to her. Once at the hospital, do not be alarmed by the people you may see in the psychiatric emergency room. Some may appear threatening or even frightening to you. Try to remember that they may be someone else's parishioners. They are indeed someone else's children. And they are all certainly God's children.

The clergyperson who is not trained in psychiatry or psychotherapy should never engage in psychotherapeutic treatment of someone with a mental illness unless the clergyperson also has the proper qualifications (for example, LCSW or MD or PsyD). This may seem objectionable to those pastoral counselors who feel competent, but people with severe mental illnesses should see a psychiatrist who can administer medication if needed and who can keep an eye on the patient's progress. This is true even if the patient sees someone else for therapy, such as a social worker or a psychologist.

Clergy can support the parishioner, however, by meeting regularly in pastoral care or spiritual direction. The process of therapy itself can be disorienting. Because therapy is often done from a secular perspective, spiritual issues may arise that the therapist may not be trained to handle. If the parishioner invites you to engage in this way, consider yourself part of the therapeutic team, but never attempt to handle such a case all by yourself. You must not attempt to fill the role of psychiatrist or therapist. You have your own role. It is extremely important that your pastoral care embrace also the patient's family.

What if your friend is battling mental illness? The most useful thing you can do as a friend is to keep in consistent contact with her. The patient will find comfort in knowing that her friend remains a friend even despite her mental illness. A phone call, a lunch date, or even an email can bolster a sagging mood. Don't expect your friend, however, to be fun to be with. Mental illnesses can make people very un-fun to be with. It is important to realize that your friend's poor mental health may look like rejection of friendship, but this is most probably not the case. She just has a sick brain. Hang in there with her.

Children should be allowed to have a role in comforting a mentally ill parent. However, most children tend to think that a parent's illness (of any kind) is their own fault. This is dangerous in turn for the child's mental health and spiritual well-being. The parent who is ill must not blame herself for her child's difficulties. At the same time it is important to recognize the children's needs. It may even be helpful to permit the children age-appropriate roles in caring for the ill parent. This can give the children a sense of contributing a degree of control in a potentially disorienting situation. Once we realized it was best to be open with them, our own children had their own roles in helping Mommy. This gave them a sense of power in an otherwise uncontrollable situation. My daughter at age three read fluently. She would read to me on the couch, on the bed, anywhere it was quiet and warm. This was somewhat of an annoyance, to tell the truth, because I just wanted to be left alone, but I knew it was important for her to play an active role in helping Mommy feel better. My son and I would sometimes play quietly with Legos. This was not easy for me either, but I knew he enjoyed playing, and it made our relationship seem somewhat more "normal." I must quickly emphasize that children should be explicitly and verbally reminded that they are not the parent and that they are not responsible for their sick parent's well-being. Reassure your children that the doctors are taking care of Mommy and that Mommy is still the Mommy.

You may also need to consider putting the children in therapy. I know this may sound over the top if you are not used to the idea of therapy. But a family with an ill parent is like a car with one flat tire. The flat tire throws the whole vehicle out of kilter. Some people may also choose family therapy and/or couples therapy. We found all of these extremely important at different times throughout my episodes.

When the situation involves an ill pastor or priest who refuses to accept the fact that she is exhibiting symptoms, it can be very difficult for the congregation to confront her. Parishioners may recognize unusual behavior in their pastor or priest but may take it personally instead of discerning possible symptoms and speaking the truth in love. Sometimes pastors and priests have difficulty allowing themselves to be pastored. I think they often rely on the power of helping others in order to feel good about themselves. But when pastors have needs they subconsciously feel should be met by their parishioners, the result is usually disastrous. Unfortunately, denominations that have no place for the office of the bishop sometimes have few ready means for pastoring, disciplining, or removing clergy. If there is a bishop, contact the bishop. If not, contact the appropriate judicatory.

Being a friend or pastor to a mentally ill individual can be difficult. Because of the stigma of mental illness, the ill person may not feel able to open up to you. Do not be offended. Be consistent in your concern, prayer, and gentle inquiries. Let them know that your friendship and care as a clergyperson is unconditional. And remember, since mental illness can be a terminal disease, you may be helping even to save a life.

13

Choosing Therapy

Protect me, O God, for I take refuge in you;
  I have said to the LORD, "You are my Lord,
  my good above all other."

Psalm 16:1

A segment of Christianity in America still is afraid of psycho-therapy, especially that conducted by secular therapists.[1] Christians may tend to turn away from psychotherapy out of lack of trust. The secular therapist often approaches religion from a worldview that is foreign to the Christian. This secular worldview in the West tends to be informed by, at some level and in addition to others, Sigmund Freud (1856–1939), Karl Marx (1818–83), and Ludwig Feuerbach (1804–72). Freud believed that religion is, among other things, a crutch to help us deal with the ultimate reality of our death. Marx saw religion as the opiate of the masses, used by those in power to control others. Feuerbach understood God to be simply "man writ large" and projected onto a cosmic screen. This reminds me of the scene in the Wizard of Oz where the Wizard's

149

true identity as an old man is revealed as Toto pulls aside the curtain around him. Certainly Freud, Marx, and Feuerbach are not the only voices informing modern secular psychotherapies. Nevertheless, their views are influential and even underlie much of contemporary Christian theology.

It is therefore sometimes claimed that the only appropriate therapist for a Christian is another Christian. The argument goes that since a non-Christian therapist will have a foreign worldview, there will be no bridge in communication between the therapist and patient. I do not necessarily agree. I do believe that it is highly important for the Christian to have a therapist who is not antagonistic to the Christian faith, but finding a secular therapist who is open enough to the Christian's worldview is not impossible. In some cases it may be a challenge.

Indeed, Christians sometimes reject therapy *in toto*, claiming that all they need for mental health is Jesus, and then things will be fine. I once had a student who interpreted her depression as a preconversion illness that disappeared upon her turning to Christ. Maybe so, but what about those of us who have a vibrant faith and a strong relationship with Jesus and yet are still thrown into the pit? Surely the voice of the psalmist throughout the Psalter reflects the plight of the poor, the outcast, and those who suffer illnesses.

A friend told me recently that it is a betrayal of one's confession of Christ to seek psychiatric help or therapy of any kind. This seems to be a not uncommon perception, especially among evangelical and orthodox Christians. Why is this so? Do we not believe that Satan can work through the biochemistry of our brain, our family relationships, our childhood, our self-image, to undo us? Satan takes advantage of whatever is at hand to set us off. So why shouldn't God be able to use a psychiatrist, even an atheist psychiatrist, to help in the healing process? Maybe the assumption is that God is not capable of this. I don't see why God's grace cannot come in the form of a daily dosage of antidepressant or in the form of a therapist, even an atheist. That cannot be impossible, surely.

You know the old joke. The drowning man sees a surfer going by who leans out with a hand extended. "Hang on, I'll get you to safety!" the surfer says.

"No," replies the floundering man, "God will save me!"

Next comes a sailboat, and a ring attached to a line is tossed out. "Hang on, we'll get you to safety!"

"No," replies the floundering man, "God will save me!"

Finally, a helicopter appears hovering overhead, and a line is let down. "Hang on, we'll get you to safety!" shouts a voice from above.

"No," replies the floundering man, "God will save me!"

Thereupon the man drowns. At the pearly gates, he meets St. Peter and asks accusingly why God did not save him from drowning. Peter replies, "Look, we sent you a surfer, a sailboat, and a helicopter. What more did you want?"

Maybe at the heart of the objection to therapy is that we are ashamed to admit that we can't handle illness, especially mental illness, on our own. It can be a devastating blow to one's sense of self, after all, to admit to mental unrest. But when we have a bad cough, we are usually not ashamed. Why are we ashamed when the problem is in our brain? Or why, when we are mentally ill, should we not react with the same dispatch in calling the doctor as we would if we find a lump in the breast?

The answer is, of course, because of the stigma involved. But what makes us think the Christian can or should be able to handle such difficulties alone, much less any other difficulty? The assumption that one can go it alone is at heart Pelagianism. This was like the position of a certain theologian, Pelagius, in the fifth century, whom Augustine tried to correct by saying that grace is solely God's doing and we cannot even take on our own the first steps toward God's saving will. According to Augustine, Pelagius shrank the grace of God.

I once heard a psychiatrist disaffected from his own field say that "God is the best psychotherapist available." I steamed at hearing that. God is no psychotherapist, except only in the broad etymological sense: God heals (*therapeuō*) our souls (*psychē*). But God heals souls only because God is the One who creates the soul in the first place. God is in this respect quite unlike any therapist I know! Expecting God to be like a psychotherapist is in fact sacrilege, blasphemy. God is not a tool to be used to meet our needs. God does, however, give us tools. Like psychotherapists, psychiatrists, medications, hospitals, not to mention surfboards, sailboats, and helicopters.

How many therapists and psychiatrists have treated me? The first was a warm and patient intern, a student of psychiatry finishing her training at the Yale Student Health Services. She arranged for my treatment for the whole academic year. This meant convincing her supervising doctor to waive the policy which would have allowed me only six weeks' treatment. Dr. E. was not a practicing Christian as far as I knew, but she tried to be sympathetic to my religious language. Yet I remember her asking me in a dubious manner whether or not I believed that the tongues of fire on the apostles at Pentecost were "real." What did "real" mean, I asked. My response probably made her question my sanity even more. I do think, though, that she understood that my religious life was not just a small part of me. I missed her greatly when I graduated from Yale and was no longer able to be seen at the Health Services.

Then I saw Dr. S., whose office was full of lush green plants but whose heart seemed hardened to anything religious, including me. It appeared that he disdained me. If you see a therapist who you feel has this sort of attitude about you, first discuss your feelings about this with him or her. Then, if you still feel disrespected and nothing changes, you might want to move on to another therapist or psychiatrist. The therapeutic relationship may simply not be viable. "Why is it important that I should be sympathetic with your religious life?" Such psychobabble. *Only because it is my entire world, you creep.* Here is an example of a secular therapist who can be damaging to the Christian. I wanted to believe that anybody of any background should be able to engage a Christian in therapy. I no longer think that. Therapists who are dogmatically

Feuerbachian, who believe that God is "man writ large," will simply not be able to get far with the Christian who disagrees, unless the therapist is very disciplined in suspending their own worldview at least for the duration of the therapeutic session. If they cannot do this, they may cause the Christian patient much psychological and spiritual pain.

Then I moved on to an LCSW (licensed clinical social worker), a caring and empathic woman who has fought hard with me and for me over the last nine years, even and especially when I just wanted her to give up. B. has been my adviser and my enemy, my blessing and my bane. There were times I just wanted her to give up on me, but of course she would not. I have been deeply grateful for her gentle yet firm care.

As I found out only after beginning therapy with her, B. is a Christian of my own denomination, although I do not know the extent of her personal religious life. She has a graduate theological education from the same institution where I received mine, so we have a common vocabulary. I feel for the most part free to talk about any religious matters, even though she clearly does not agree with me on all topics. Who would? But our therapy is not "Christian" in orientation. She does not pray with me, although she has said that she does pray for all of her patients outside the context of the therapeutic session. ("How could I take care of all of you all alone?") She does not encourage or discourage any particular set of religious or spiritual practices for the healing of mental illness. While she is not a "Christian therapist," she is a therapist who is a Christian and a person of prayer. I feel that God has clearly drawn me into her orbit for healing. She is my angel of mercy.

After I left Dr. S., I was receiving medication for depression from my general practitioner. When I slipped into hypomania, B. recognized the symptoms and insisted that I see a psychiatrist for medication. Apparently the antidepressant had tipped me from depression to hypomania, but the general practitioner did not catch the signs. This is why I believe that a psychiatrist, not a general practitioner, should handle medical management, even if the patient does not see the psychiatrist for psychotherapy. Psychiatrists are much more aware of the side effects of medications than are general practitioners and know what to look for in their patients' affect. I do wonder if I would have tipped into hypomania if a psychiatrist and not a general practitioner had been managing my medication. Maybe a psychiatrist would have been able to identify the signs at the very beginning of the hypomania. B. was very wise to refer me to a psychiatrist immediately.

"Nobody doesn't like Dr. K." Well, I must have been the first of the nobodies. He was all right at first: very kind and caring, with a good sense of humor. He even would go overtime if I was particularly distressed, something that most psychiatrists' schedules will not allow. While he seemed at first to accept my religious makeup, even if he clearly could not understand, he commented one day that I had better not try to interpret my illness through religious language. He said it with a little snort.

While Dr. K. was compassionate for the most part, I began to feel less and less confident about his care over time. His office looked like the ill-fated *Titanic*: haphazard stacks of files sliding across the floor, papers spilling out. Who is not being helped here? What—or who—is falling through the cracks? I soon found that I was one of those people. When Dr. Disorganization could not be reached and did not renew necessary prescriptions during two medical crises, I found another psychiatrist. It is wrenching to take leave of a psychiatrist or therapist, even when you know you have to. So I had to wait until I was feeling well enough to do so. I suppose Dr. K. thought that I had forgotten his neglect of my care. Instead, I had begun to feel strong enough to go elsewhere.

Now I see the psychiatrist who administered my ECT in the hospital. I see him for a fifteen-minute session every six weeks for medication, and, unlike with Dr. K., the insurance covers the sessions except for a small copay. Dr. O. looks like Einstein. White hair everywhere. He has a zany bike with a chair for a seat and the front wheel extended far forward from the frame. He rides it all over town, to the hospital, to the office. He too is caring and compassionate, if self-avowedly eccentric. He also has a good sense of humor, an important characteristic for me in a doctor. Dr. O. has brought up religion on occasion, joking for instance about the trouble that the Episcopal Church has had since voting at General Convention in 2003 to consecrate a "practicing" openly gay bishop. I immediately shut off discussion, telling him he wouldn't understand. "But psychiatrists are supposed to understand!" I coughed.

Then there were all the doctors and social workers and nurses in the hospitals who have treated me. For the most part they followed a strictly medical model, not even offering therapy. I received little therapy at Yale Psychiatric Institute, so the staff's attitude toward the religious life did not come out much. But they were amused that I was trying so hard to say Morning and Evening Prayer. I think they may even have been a bit concerned.

Another social worker whom I saw with the whole family was an excellent therapist. He saw the family in different constellations: the children, Matthew and me, all four of us, Matthew alone, but not me alone. He respected my therapeutic relationship with B. and didn't want to muddy the waters there. As far as I could tell, he was not a practicing Christian, but he tried hard at least to respect my religious life. C. was very insightful, practical, and didn't waste any time with us. He is an instance of a social worker whom I would recommend to any parishioner, even though I do not know his personal belief system. He is able to keep it appropriately under wraps.

I now am engaged in a therapy group in addition to seeing B. The facilitator of the group is a religiously observant Jew. S. is quite open to questions of religious life and the relationship between that and mental health. She sees this to be a positive relationship. She believes that a patient's religious life does not necessarily fight against, but rather can promote, mental health. Even though she is clearly of another religious tradition, she is respectful of the faith of those in the group, several of whom are Christians.

This is part of the reason I am absolutely unconvinced by those who say that Christians must see only Christian therapists. What is, after all, a Christian therapist? A Christian who happens to be a therapist? A therapist who happens to be a Christian? A therapist who uses Christian concepts, practices, and scriptures in the context of therapy? What would these be? As in the case of S., a therapist of another religion can be just as supportive and understanding of religious life and experience. As in the case of C., a therapist may be religiously neutral and still be able to help devout Christians in profound ways. The most important piece of advice I would give is that the Christian patient should look for a therapist with whom the patient feels comfortable and respected both personally and spiritually.

> I have set before you life and death, blessings and curses. Choose life so that you and your descendants may live, loving the LORD your God, obeying him, and holding fast to him; for that means life to you and length of days.
>
> Deuteronomy 30:19–20

If you, my reader, are feeling that you may be experiencing symptoms of mental illness (see appendix II for a quick checklist), do not wait to get help. The whole syndrome or set of symptoms may only get worse if left unaddressed. As a friend once encouraged me, referring to the practice of the colonial soldiers at the attack of the British, don't wait until you see the whites of their eyes. Shoot as soon as you see the red of their coats. If you or anyone you know is experiencing symptoms of mental illness, seek help right away. There is so much help out there, and as the psalmist knows, praising God is the purpose of our life. Who will give God thanks in the grave? Anything we can use to get out and stay out of that grave is a good thing.

In the end, we should consider engaging in secular therapy not as a threat from the outside but as spoiling the gold of the Egyptians. Just as Moses and his band were told to take from the riches of the Egyptians, so the Christian should feel unconstrained to borrow from secular wisdom in the healing of mental illnesses. The

Christian should bear in mind that this spoiling of the Egyptians can be good and proper, as long as the "Egyptian" doesn't try to tear at the gold and injure the fleeing Hebrew. Trust is necessary for the therapeutic relationship to bring healing. Any feeling of distrust will break apart the relationship.

Therefore, when you choose a therapist, do so carefully. Interview two or three therapists. Check out each therapist's office. What does it tell you about him or her? Is it neat and organized? Is it a mess? Do you care? Ask about anything you feel matters to you. For me it was the therapists' degrees and experience in therapy, how they felt about religious patients, if they had any understanding of Christianity, and so on. Do they answer these questions eagerly, or do they want to know why you are asking? This last strategy may be a huge cop-out on the part of a psychotherapist. However, it can also be a useful tactic to get you to say more. And maybe that is what you need to be doing. But if you want answers to your questions, stick to your guns. Do you feel respected? Comfortable? Is there a good rapport? The most important part of your work together will come from the relationship itself, so choose someone with whom you feel most likely to have a good therapeutic relationship.

Ultimately, the best therapeutic relationship will be based on trust. This is why it depends entirely on the match between therapist and patient rather than religious issues or educational credentials alone. And if you are looking for someone to pray with you and for you, I would advise that you seek out either clergy or a spiritual director to be another party in your therapeutic team.

I should add a word about therapy itself. It is not an easy road. You will have to face events and facts about your life, your family, and your choices that you might rather not have to face. Rather than feeling "therapeutic," it may, especially at first, make you feel torn up inside. For example, being reminded of the anniversary of any death can be literally sickening, and this can come up in therapy: the sane mind can become clouded at the remembrance of such pain. Anniversaries of tragedies can be all the more painful.

Anyone in this position might have to take a day off to recuperate. Anniversaries of suicides may be that much harder still. The painful memories of the person who took their own earthly life never leave you. And therapy usually leads you to remember and face such things.

You may have to go through a few therapists until you find one whom you can trust, with whom you feel comfortable. And if your insurance won't cover it, it can be quite expensive. Choosing against therapy on account of expense is usually more expensive in the long run than engaging in therapy would have been in the first place.

As you look for a mental health professional, you may need a psychiatrist who can prescribe medication. This is a doctor with an MD, and sometimes also a PhD in a related field. You may prefer a licensed counselor (LPC) or a social worker (LCSW) or a psychologist (PsyD) for therapy. These usually do not prescribe medicine, so you will also need a psychiatrist for medical management. A social worker can be less expensive and better skilled in therapy than a psychiatrist, although this entirely depends upon the individual practitioner. There are also various kinds of "pastoral counselors," some of whom may advertise themselves as Christians. They may not necessarily have a degree in counseling, so ask. In some states, just about anybody can hang out their shingle as a "therapist."

Conclusion

This is my comfort in my trouble,
that your promise gives me life. . . .
It is good for me that I have been afflicted,
that I might learn your statutes.

Psalm 119:50, 71

Is it *good* for me that I have been afflicted? Isn't there an easier
way to learn God's statutes? How can I agree with the psalmist
here? In the midst of all my ills, I can honestly say that God has
taught me in his mercy and despite my misery.

One of the things that God in his mercy has taught me from
my illness has been about the nature of Christian marriage. Illnesses, especially mental illnesses, can either destroy a marriage
or cement it. In my case my marriage was strengthened.

I remember when I married at age twenty-two that the traditional vows meant much to me. But when it came to "in sickness
and in health," I always thought I was promising to take care of
my new husband. It did not occur to me that I would need to be
taken care of. It did not enter my mind that I might be the weak
one someday, that I would need to accept my husband's love in

a new way. I had never thought that life's circumstances might render us no longer equals in the give and take of unconditional love. I was young and naive.

Of course, when we marry, we cannot foresee the blessings and the curses we may encounter in life. Hence the vows. Otherwise it would be easy to say to ourselves that our spouse "just isn't the person I married." And of course, Matthew could easily have said that of me.

> Love's not love that alters when it alteration finds.
>
> Shakespeare (1564–1606)

But Matthew taught me how to accept love when I could not give it. This was a hard lesson indeed for me. He taught me of the wonders of grace, of the unconditional love of the marriage covenant. Because he hung on and was a rock-solid helpmeet to me, because he looked on tempest and was not shaken, I learned after my recovery the power of Christian marriage to bear it out to the edge of doom.

I thought, of course, when I made those vows as a relative youngster, that I knew what Shakespeare's sonnet meant about bearing it out to the edge of doom. Like Jesus asks Peter in the old hymn: "Are you ready, said the Master, to be crucified with me?" Peter's voice answers "Yes!" Now, what did Peter really know about being crucified with Jesus? How dare he say yes? And how dare we take these vows? Christian marriage is a crucible for the formation of Christ in us, with its daily crucifixions to self and its daily resurrections of love in the bonds of affection. And even without affection. I sincerely wanted to make the vows, and I meant them, but I did not fully understand the implications of what I was saying. That is part of why people get "cold feet" at the altar. But I am so grateful for those vows, and for the husband God gave me. He is my best friend. We now know what is worth fighting over: precious little. And if, God forbid, Matthew should become ill, I pray that I can be such a bulwark to him as he was and continues to be to me.

Another thing I learned was a deep compassion for the sick, bed-ridden, and homeless that I did not have before. I always thought I was a person of deep compassion, but I see now that this was not true. Sometimes suffering is the only way to learn true compassion, true "feeling with." How, after all, can one put oneself into the shoes of another who is suffering without having suffered personally? I don't think that I would have agreed with this before. I simply thought that one could just imagine the other's hell. I no longer think this.

I realize that I myself could easily have become homeless if I had not had the support of my husband. I was incapable of earning a living, incapable of the basic tasks of daily life, paying bills, putting together a meal. Now I look at the homeless with a new sense of compassion, indeed respect. I now understand why some talk to themselves and are irritable and jumpy and odd, or semi-comatose and unkempt. So many homeless are mentally ill, or addicts from self-medication, or both. The constant stress of being homeless could easily bring on a mental illness. Or the illness could cause the homelessness in the first place: a vicious cycle. Even though I have never been an addict or homeless, I see myself in these people. I see them in me.

When I visit the sick, I see my own mortality. Most of us tend to ignore or forget the fragility of life when we are healthy. One of the elderly whom I visit, a stroke patient, sometimes tries to talk, but he falls asleep readily while trying. His brain is very sick. His mind must also be compromised. But his soul? Certainly not. That is why his son has a hard time knowing when to let go. "Is it hard to keep your eyes open?" I ask. He sleeps. How agonizingly difficult it is to be sick. His frailty reminds me that I too will someday sleep in death. I anoint him with holy oil, beseeching God the Father, God the Son, and God the Holy Spirit to grant him peace. "The grass withers, the flower fades; but the word of our God will stand forever" (Isa. 40:8).

To mark your own mortality before the Almighty is to acknowledge his sovereignty, his abiding mercy and grace. It is easy to forget

God's sovereignty when one is healthy and seemingly powerful. We usually assume that we have all the time in the world. "So teach us to number our days that we may apply our hearts to wisdom" (Ps. 90:12). In a sense this is what we do in our Lenten disciplines: number our days. My life these past years has been one long Lent, out of which I hope has come a resurrection of compassion.

I also learned that sick people are not necessarily weak. I am ashamed to admit that I did not already know this. Sick people are afflicted. They need the help of the Christian community, not our rejection. Mentally ill people can shock us. The stigma of mental illness can turn us off. But it should be the Christian community of all places where those who suffer are welcomed and supported, prayed for and comforted.

I learned what faith means even in abandonment, especially in abandonment. Even in my very great suffering, when prayer was shouting blasphemies at God and I felt completely abandoned, somehow deep down I knew that Jesus was with me, even if in an absent way. I saw the backside of God, as Moses did hiding in the cleft of the rock. And maybe this is all I could take. After all, not many see the face of God and live (Exod. 33:17–23). Seeing the backside of God is incredibly painful, but I experienced God even if only in his absence while I was ill.

And even in my abandonment, I remembered even if only fog-gily that God had good plans for me (Jer. 29:11), plans for welfare and not for evil, *to give me a future and a hope*. It was painful to remember this, and I had to keep reminding myself over and over. At that time, I really did imagine God as a huge cat and myself as a helpless mouse being batted back and forth by God's paws. When will God stop playing with me like this? *God has plans for your welfare and not for evil, to give you a future and a hope*. Please give me that future now, I prayed. I had to have patience when every ounce of my flesh fought for immediate health, which was denied me. Faith can be this sort of patience, a hanging on when God's glory is not felt or sensed. Faithfulness in this context truly makes God's face beam.

Sometimes I wonder if I will miss my tribulations. I have not known the severe pain of my brain disorder now for over two years. However, it remains a part of my life. The analogy the doctor has given me is that my disease is like diabetes: there is no cure, but with care there is a way to treat it so that it is not terminal. I still must take my medication faithfully, avoiding the foods that interact with it. I must make sure to exercise every day, to see my therapists and doctors, to allow for this invasion into my life. Yet without the pain, I do learn less about faith, about the nature of faithfulness, about my own weaknesses and God's strength. I am so relieved, however, to have returned from among the tombs. I have my memories, which will continue to teach me.

> Why are you cast down, O my soul?
> And why are you disquieted within me?
> Hope in God; for I shall again praise him, my help and my
> God.
>
> Psalms 42 and 43 RSV

I learned during these years to pray. It was not as if I had never prayed before. As with learning compassion, which I thought I already knew, I learned how to pray. The Daily Office helped with this, in its forms for prayer and its place for intercessory prayer. However, it was more than just this. Prayer from a mentally ill mind is exceedingly difficult. Not only is it hard to concentrate, a faculty necessary for prayer. It is actually painful to give thanks. Which means one has to try all the harder, or maybe not at all. To let the Holy Spirit pray through you is a form of prayerful surrender.

I knew from Scripture that to be faithful one has to hope in God and praise God, but how could I do that now? Not, certainly, on my own. I strapped myself to the prayers and praises of Israel, the Scriptures, and relied on the prayers of others, from ancient Israel to my present-day parish and family. We sometimes forget the importance of intercessory prayer, but we must remember that sometimes we may be praying for someone who simply cannot pray for themselves. I learned that prayer does not always feel good, that it may be more like scaling a steep wall than walking on a level plain. The old saying fits: "If the mountain were smooth, you couldn't climb it." I learned that we must always pray, even and especially when we don't feel like it or when it feels compulsory and rote and dry.

When an acquaintance had bone cancer, his friends stood around him and exclaimed how he was so courageous and faithful. He would look shocked and say that he had no faith, no courage. Being ill does not necessarily make one virtuous. I know now how he felt. Friends would tell me what a witness I was to the grace of God. Of course I did not feel myself to be any such witness. I just knew that I had to make it through my own trials. "My brothers and sisters, whenever you face trials of any kind, consider it nothing but joy" (James 1:2).

A dear friend made me a prie-dieu for my ordination. It stands in my office, holding a prayer book and a Bible. Whenever I say prayers while kneeling at that beautiful handmade piece of art, my soul is humbled and lifted at the same time. How could anyone make such an object for me? Partly out of friendship, and partly because he knows that as a priest I have a responsibility to pray on behalf of the community of faith. Thanks be to God that through the mire and clay, now I truly can pray, and more deeply than ever before.

I also learned something very deep about the Christian life: even for all that pain, I would not give it up for what I learned through it. I had known before in my head that joy is different from happiness. But now the difference is engraved on my heart. Sometimes we will be simply unhappy, and sometimes very unhappy indeed, but the joy of the LORD is our strength (Neh. 8:10). Joy comes not from the vicissitudes of daily circumstance as does happiness. It comes to us from the deep calling to deep, God's voice to us as we hear it in Scripture and sacrament. God in his providence weaves joy into our lives despite the suffering. Sometimes even through the suffering.

O Lord, my heart is not lifted up,
　　my eyes are not raised too high;
I do not occupy myself with things
　　too great and too marvelous for me.
But I have calmed and quieted my soul,
　　like a child quieted at her mother's breast,
　　like a child that is quieted is my soul.
O Israel, hope in the Lord
　　from this time forth and for evermore.

　　　　　　　　　　　　　　　　Psalm 131 RSV

This psalm goes from individual lament to corporate hope and praise. And this is the journey of our lives before God, proceeding from our laments to praises of the God of Israel. This is not sticky-sweet pablum given as though to compensate for the pain; it is the very life of Jesus poured out for us. Joy comes from the crucified and risen Jesus, not from our inner psyche.

This is why, as I have said, the personality matters relatively little to our lives before God. Especially when a person is mentally ill, the personality, the outward affect, can change. Our affect and desire may change. But no matter how fickle our hearts and minds may be, God is constant. God is faithful even though we are changing or changed. And this is a source of joy.

I also learned that despair is not the chief sin for the mentally ill. Despair is a reaction to evil, to the forces that work against God's good creation and providence. Despair may be involuntary, caused by a brain disorder. Or it may be voluntary, caused by giving in under the burden of too much pain. But it is always a reaction to some form of evil, some deprivation of the good, and is understandable as such. This is an exceedingly important lesson: *despair can live with Christian faith*. Indeed, having despair while knowing in your heart that God has conquered even that is a great form of faith tried by fire.

And the counterpart to despair is hope. This kind of hope is not merely optimism, which looks to the present with a cheery face. Christian hope looks to the future, to God's promise of the resurrection. This is God's act alone, turning around of all things back to God. "If for this life only we have hoped in Christ, we are of all people most to be pitied" (1 Cor. 15:19). It is this promised future that redeems our present and allows us to have hope beyond mere optimism. Hope is not a subjective feeling but an objective knowledge of God's being, act, and identity. Therefore even those with mental illnesses who cannot "feel" hope must be reassured of its objectivity—an important role for the Christian friend. "Hope that is seen is not hope" (Rom. 8:24). In God's good time, in the heavenly Jerusalem, there will be no more tears. God himself will wipe them away. "Weeping may spend the night, but joy comes in the morning" (Ps. 30:6).

With the apostle Paul, who certainly had his own difficulties in his ministry, I have learned to say,

> In all these things we are more than conquerors through him who loved us. For I am convinced that neither death, nor life, nor angels, nor rulers, nor things present, nor things to come, nor powers, nor height, nor depth, nor anything else in all creation, will be able to separate us from the love of God in Christ Jesus our Lord.
>
> Romans 8:37–39

Nothing in all of creation will be able to separate us from the love of God. Not death nor dwelling on death. Not illness that even makes us turn away at times from God and from life. We are conquerors through him who loved us, Jesus Christ. Even in the midst of illness, and even mental illness, to know that we are conquerors leads to health. Who says, after all, that Christian faith perpetuates psychological illness?

Thirteen years now after my diagnosis of major depression and seven years after my diagnosis with bipolar disorder, after good and bad times, I have now had two good years. Two years of solid improvement, working again at full steam, being able to talk to people without pain, smiling without feeling that my face will crack. I do not anticipate the coming day with dread, nor do I fear hypomanic episodes. I suppose all of this could recur, but I have a new confidence that if it does, it will not crush me as it did. For now it seems more like Jesus has chased it away, with the help of medicine and therapy, a loving family, and supportive friends.

> "See, the home of God is among mortals.
> He will dwell with them as their God;
> they will be his peoples
> and God himself will be with them;
> he will wipe away every tear from their eyes.
> Death will be no more;
> mourning and crying and pain will be no more,
> for the first things have passed away."

And the one who was seated on the throne said, "See, I am making all things new."

Revelation 21:3–5

See, I am making all things new. This is the message of the redemption we have in Christ Jesus. In the New Jerusalem, there will be no more crying or pain. These things will have passed away, because the One who rules, who sits on the throne, has conquered it all. Of course, this happens at the end time, when Jesus comes back to reign definitively over all powers. Until then, we do have tears, we do suffer, we do confront our own deaths. But the promise given those in Christ is that God will make all things new beyond death, tears, and illness.

TRANSFIGURATION 2005

Afterword to the Second Edition

I have been surprised and overjoyed to find that this book has ministered to so many people. I had been hoping that churches and seminaries would find it useful for the practice and teaching of pastoral care, and this has indeed been the case. It has also been adopted for courses in both systematic theology and biblical interpretation in colleges and universities in the United States, Canada, and the United Kingdom. I was delighted to hear that it was also being used in two medical schools and one nursing school, in psychiatric hospitals, a prison ministry, and an Army chaplaincy in Iraq. A colleague used it in her book on Christian identity as an example of how and why Christian doctrine "matters." It has been translated into Chinese. I am gratified that my work has borne fruit.

Developments in Diagnosis and Treatments

Readers should be aware that since I wrote this book, the Diagnostic Statistical Manual (which was at the time DSM-IV) has been updated. The DSM is the official guidebook for the diagnosis of psychiatric diseases. At the time of my writing this afterword, the current version is DSM-V. The update to the current edition was not without controversy for many reasons, only one of which was a concern that the reclassification of diseases could jeopardize the health-care coverage of some disorders and therefore of some patients.

Also since I wrote the first edition, treatments have changed somewhat. Medications have entered the scene that were only at the research stage eight years ago. One promising medication for depression still in studies is Ketamine, and a few others are already available by prescription. Newer non-medication therapies are beginning to become more available, such as transcranial direct current stimulation (tDCS), repetitive transcranial magnetic stimulation (rTMS), vagus nerve stimulation (VNS), and deep brain stimulation (DBS). Older non-medication therapies, such as electroconvulsive therapy (ECT), are becoming less stigmatized and more accepted among patients. Other therapies long respected are now being offered in easily accessible and popular forms, such as paperbacks and workbook editions. This is true especially for cognitive behavioral therapy (CBT) and dialectical behavioral therapy (DBT). Resilience has become an important concept in therapeutic research.

Some of the older medications, which until recently had been considered "outdated," are making a comeback, but in different dosages and for other disorders than was previously the case. Groundbreaking research has pointed to genetic links between different types of brain diseases. This itself may lead to the development of new treatments. The Broad Institute, a biomedical research center, with its $650 million donation specifically for psychiatric research from the Stanley Family Foundation, is also a beacon of hope offering cutting-edge studies into the genesis and treatment of brain disorders.

The work of the National Alliance on Mental Illness (NAMI) continues its work to diminish the stigma of mental illness. NAMI has expanded its programs to reach into minority and under-served communities and to multiple faith communities. The tragedies of suicide in the families of high-profile evangelical church leaders are also forcing Christians to speak about mental illness who might otherwise have been ashamed to voice their suffering. It is horrific that it should take such senseless loss to force us to deal with this difficult subject, yet at the very least some blessing may rise from these tragedies. In the wake of their suicides, celebrities such as David Foster Wallace and Robin Williams have also left at least the possibility of public discussion of suicide prevention.

Addressing Readers' Comments

On Reading Scripture

One reader commented that appendix I on "Why and How I Read Scripture" is too short. He wanted me to explain why I don't use more conventional approaches from the world of academia to read the Bible, such as historical criticisms of various sorts. The fact is, however, that I do use historical-critical methods. I find them very helpful in illuminating the biblical text. I will quickly add that those methods alone do fall short in building the kind of faithfully nourishing reading that helped me survive the episodes of my illness. But that is no reason not to use historical-critical methods.

These methods often do not assist the use of the imagination in worship or the role of the will in praise. Historical-critical methods, of course, have no pretense to this. I therefore often find helpful some of the traditional methods of interpretation. One rabbinic view is that biblical interpretation is like turning a diamond, slowly refracting the light through its planes into the many colors of the rainbow. Some of the interpretive methods embraced by the early and medieval church are like this. They sought multiple levels of meaning and allowed the interpreter greater freedom. The creativity and spiritual nourishment that flow from this freedom is one place where I find the Holy Spirit entering into our readings of Scripture.

But these interpreters are sometimes accused of endlessly distorting the sense of a text, threatening an "objective" reading. This was a stock Reformation charge against Catholic interpreters: they were turning Scripture into a "wax nose," which could be molded at will. But the early church acknowledged clear boundaries marking off what was allowable and what was transgressive in interpretation of Scripture. The act and fruits of interpretation were to be restrained by the Rule of Faith and the Rule of Love. Any interpretation that worked against the building up of faith and love was not a proper reading.

The use of these Rules in the act of interpreting Scripture is understood by most historical-critical readers to be quaint at best. But the kind of reading that enabled me to survive during my darkest times embraces the text as three dimensional, a world into which the reader enters in communion with the Body of Christ. This invites the reader into the very life of God and allows her to call God into her life, inviting God into her pain. It allows her to seek and find her place within that world, to hear the text as divine address. But I have written about the interpretation of Scripture in many other places.[1] Lest I bore my readers who may be uninterested in such things, I will refrain from going further here.

On Inclusive Language

One reader expressed anger over my approach to inclusive language. She declared it "too conservative" and gave up reading the book even before finishing the introduction. I want to address this as briefly as possible. For some it may not be brief enough. If this is too pedantic for you, I invite you to skip to my third response.

Readers who are not churchgoers in the First World may not be familiar with the orthodoxy which has gained ascent over the past few decades. The current defining and delimiting of how we are to refer to God and to humans is in places openly codified, as in some seminaries and chaplaincies, and in other places simply assumed. It has become axiomatic that masculine and/or hierarchical terms for God are no longer to be used in scholarly Scripture translations and in the liturgies of many mainline denominations. The terms *Lord*, *King*, *Master*, and *Father* are now rejected in favor of more gender-inclusive terms. Those who do not respect these language policies tend to be met either with stony silence or open correction.

I myself question many of the foundational assumptions about the relationship between God and humanity held by inclusive-language proponents. But I have written about this also at length elsewhere and will simply say that I have not significantly changed my mind on these issues.[2] I would therefore ask your patience and forbearance when you do not agree with me. The suffering of those who live with mental illness is great. I ask that you focus on the subject matter at hand and read with charity rather than walk away in offense.

On Genre

Other readers were not comfortable with the fact that the book does not fit neatly into any one genre or category. One person understood the book to be a memoir, another thought it was a manual on pastoral care, and yet another hailed it as a spiritual road map for patient and family. It is none of these. If it does fit a genre, I might say it is a theodicy, but that isn't a fitting description either. Theodicy as a philosophical question dwells at the level of theory. There is nothing wrong per se with theories about God's relation to human suffering, unless you are in the midst of suffering, in which case theories are the last thing you need. Don't try to give a theory to someone at the window ledge ready to jump.

Darkness does indeed ask questions about God's relation to human suffering, but from within a specific context: the life of one Christian trying to live faithfully with—and in spite of—the suffering of a mental illness. The larger concern is not philosophical or theoretical. The framework here in which the questions are asked and lived out is classical Christian confession and devotion.

A beloved senior colleague told me that he understood the book to be an extended prayer. He said he found reading it to be a devotional experience. I take this to be the highest compliment anyone has given me. This is how I would prefer that the book be read. Yes, it contains memories, but the book is not about me, and it is not about my memories. Yes, I hope it will be useful in pastoral care, but it is no manual. Yes, I hope to give light to others who must tread this dark road after and with me. But *Darkness* is not a guidebook for pastoral care, it is not a roadmap—much less a GPS—and it is certainly no floodlight. Please don't read it that way. It simply asks questions about the specific kind of suffering of mental illness in light of faith in a merciful God. This book is not about me, you, the church, the world, or even mental illness. This book is about the triune God and how we are to live faithfully in the light of his presence even as we suffer.

On My Title

Another reader complained that the book's subtitle promises more than it delivers. She felt that it suggests falsely that the book is about mental illnesses in general when in fact the focus is on one illness: bipolar disorder. Touchée. It is true that the book has more to do with the symptoms of bipolar disorder and depression than with most of the symptoms of the other Major Mental Illnesses. But again, as I have said, the book is not fundamentally about mental illness. Maybe the title needs changing.

I myself am not entirely happy with either the title or subtitle. They might have been different if I had sat longer with them. Readers have complained that the phrase "darkness is my only companion" is such a downer. Again, touchée.

To be fair, the title comes from the final verse of Psalm 88 in the 1979 Episcopal Book of Common Prayer. Because I pray the

Psalms from the Book of Common Prayer (BCP), I memorized the verse as it is translated there: "My friend and neighbor you have put away from me, and darkness is my only companion." When I prayed the psalm, that verse rang out to me. As hard as this may be for others to understand, it even reassured me, comforted me. I felt completely alone, in pain, and in utter darkness, but that was OK. If the psalmist could cry out to God even in such misery, then it was OK for me to feel that way and to cry out as well. My complete despair was not a sign of my lack of faith. Because my cry was directed to God, it was no abdication of faith.

The negativity of my title, though, is not the fault of Psalm 88 itself but of the odd translation in the Episcopal Book of Common Prayer (1979). The BCP (1979) apparently modernized Myles Coverdale's long-cherished translation of the Psalter, which was the foundation of the classical tradition of English psalmody from the sixteenth century onward. Here is how BCP 1928, which followed Coverdale, translates Psalm 88's final verse: "My lovers and friends hast thou put away from me, and hid mine acquaintance out of my sight." As I read it, this 1928 translation comes closer to the Hebrew (MT), the Greek (LXX), and the Latin (Vulgate) than the 1979 BCP translation does.

In fact, I don't see how or why the BCP 1979 translators came to render the verse as they did. I am sure they had a reason, and I have tried to research the issue without success. Here is the last line of Psalm 88 in the RSV: "Thou hast caused lover and friend to shun me; my companions are in darkness." The NRSV is not much different: "You have caused friend and neighbor to shun me; my companions are in darkness." And in most of the other English translations I have checked, darkness itself is not the psalmist's companion. Nevertheless, this is what the BCP 1979 translation suggests.

If I were to have written the book now, I think I would have given it a title based on the first part of John 1:5, "The light shines in the darkness," or maybe Psalm 27:1 (BCP), "The LORD is my light and my salvation," or Psalm 139:11 (BCP), "Darkness is not dark to you." I would choose these, though, not so much because they are necessarily any less negative than "darkness is my only companion." I simply don't agree with the 1979 BCP choice of translation of Psalm 88:19.

On the Role of Feelings

Other readers have been confused by my claim that feelings are not central to the spiritual life of the Christian, particularly to one who struggles with poor mental health. I would like to clarify this.

While it is true that many methods of psychotherapy focus (at least in part) on feelings, they also focus on actions and memories, habits and aspirations, and the like. The Christian faith has to do with God's unitary act of healing all creation in the life, death, and resurrection of Jesus Christ. Christian devotion has to do in part with our memory of that act in Scripture: "For as often as you eat this bread and drink the cup, you proclaim the Lord's death until he comes" (1 Cor. 11:26). It has to do with our memory of that act in our worship: "We remember his death, We proclaim his resurrection, We await his coming in glory" (BCP 368). And the Christian faith has to do with our own actions based on that memory: "Love one another as I have loved you" (John 15:12). Memories and actions. The focus on feelings is at best peripheral.

Granted, there is indeed a strand of Christianity that trades on feelings. The feeling of ultimate dependence on God; the feeling of joy and elation; the feeling of happiness that comes from love toward neighbor; the feeling of thrill at financial prosperity. Some of these may be proper expressions of Christian faith; the final one is clearly not.

These feelings may seem good. But they may terrify us, or horrify us, or drive us to a dangerous level of despair, depending on our context and our experience. However we may feel about ourselves, about the world, or even about God, our feelings can neither substantiate nor falsify the gospel. And these feelings can neither substantiate nor negate our witness to God.

Some Christian communities apparently suggest that if we do not feel the joy of the Lord, we somehow have missed the mark, or that we are not saved, or that we don't believe rightly, or that we don't pray enough. This belief has dire consequences for the spiritual life of the mentally ill Christian. These claims locate the truth of the gospel in our interiority, in our subjectivity. This is dangerous.

People struggling with poor mental health sometimes simply cannot feel pleasure. The technical term for this symptom is *anhedonia*, literally, the inability to feel pleasure. But the fact that we may not be able to feel pleasure doesn't mean that God doesn't love us, or that we are lost, or that we are damned, or that if we pray harder everything will be better. Yes, feeling pleasure is wonderful, feeling that God loves us is beyond measure, and yes, prayer is crucial for the Christian life. But these are not indicators of the quality of our life before God.

It is especially important for us to remind our brothers and sisters in Christ who live with mental illness that God is objective. In other words, God is not a matter of our subjectivity. God is objectively real whether we feel his presence or not. That may sound naive philosophically, but frankly, I don't care. God does not "exist" inside us, is not inseparable from us, is not trapped within us. This is what I mean by saying that God is objectively real: God is independent of and unfettered by how we feel. We all need to be reminded of God's objectivity whether we are ill or healthy.

Underlying my readers' misunderstanding of my regard for feelings may actually be a general misunderstanding of psychotherapy itself. Or of *good* psychotherapy, anyway. I think this misunderstanding of psychotherapy is what may keep many—especially Christians—from seeking it.

One person (who clearly needed psychotherapy) told me that he did not need psychotherapy because he wasn't a "feelings" person. Maybe he thought he did not need to talk about his feelings. Or maybe he did not want to talk about his feelings. Or maybe he had no feelings to talk about. That would be impossible, because he is human. Apparently he thought that this is the only thing psychotherapy would "do": make him talk about his feelings.

It is true that good psychotherapy makes us access our feelings, communicate them, come to terms with them, and learn how they bubble up into destructive actions despite our best intentions. Good psychotherapy will help us learn how, when, and whether it might be appropriate to communicate these feelings to others. Most important, good psychotherapy seeks to help us learn how our feelings can be handled appropriately so they won't cause further pain, to us or to those we love or live with or work with. Psychotherapy is practice for life.

Psychotherapy can take more than just one form. Talk therapy relies on verbal communication. Art therapy can consist of painting, photography, and writing but can also include gardening, cooking, dance, and the like. Art therapy allows us to communicate our inner selves through creating beauty. Group therapy trains us in communicating with more than one person at the same time. Many other types of therapies help us with the relationship between communication, thought, and action. Especially here I think of cognitive behavioral therapy and dialectical behavioral therapy, but the list does not end here. The goal is to nurture healthier patterns of communicating and living in order to short circuit negative (or "maladaptive") patterns of thinking and acting. In turn, this can lessen and relieve some of the symptoms of mental illness and lift some of their burdens.

I hope this clarifies my understanding of the role of feelings, both in the Christian life and in the attempt to manage the symptoms of mental illness.

What I Have Learned Since the First Edition

The Nature of Chronic Illness

Responding to readers is relatively easy. But I find myself coming up short at the task of writing about what I have learned in my own life since the first edition of this book. In 2006 when *Darkness* first came out, I was in an open place where God had rescued me (Ps. 18:20). While I knew that I was living with a chronic illness and accepted that there was no "cure," still I was relieved to know that at least the illness could be managed. And we were doing that. Or so I thought. I soon learned that mental illnesses, like any other chronic disease, are never fixed targets at which we aim our meds and therapies. Life happens. Circumstances change. And particularly with mental illnesses, brain chemistry can shift.

As I was reviewing the proofs to the first edition of *Darkness*, my mother lay dying just feet from me on a rented hospice bed. We did not know then that my father was also dying. Dad died the evening of Friday, August 11, 2006. Mom died the following Friday evening. That week the symptoms of my illness, which I had thought were a fixed target, turned into guerilla warfare. A new battery of meds was loaded, aimed, and fired in rapid succession at my symptoms. But not much of it deterred the enemy. Some of it even backfired and wounded me.

And so I have learned what I thought I already knew: chronic disease ebbs and flows. One has episodes of illness, some less severe, some deadly. One is not always ill, but the illness never leaves. Like diabetes, mental illnesses have no cure (at present), but can often be successfully managed. But I find the comparison with diabetes unhelpful. I have thought over the years that asthma makes a better analogy. It also is a chronic illness. If left untreated, it also can be fatal. But it also can be treated and managed. In some cases, people can even outgrow asthma. One can have asthma but not always be gasping for breath. One can have a mental illness but not always be plagued by its symptoms.

Our son had asthma as a child. We had to be prepared for an attack, keeping the inhaler nearby. We played both detective and weather forecaster in order to protect him. How had his attacks come on in the past, and how could we avoid them in the future? Was a cold snap in the forecast? Add an extra layer of clothing. Were the neighbors sanding their house or blowing leaves? Don't let him play in the backyard. And so with episodes of mental illness, we have to be both detectives and weather forecasters, looking backward for clues and looking ahead for potential storms.

And yet this looking back and looking forward may be exactly what psychologists and counselors will tell us *not* to do. We are to "stay in the moment." Do not allow yourself to look behind for too long lest you get stuck in the past. Do not look too much to the future, as though you could flee the present. A wise friend once gave me an adage he had learned from Alcoholics Anonymous: "If you keep one foot in the past and one foot in the future, you pee all over the present." So very true.

However, like other chronic diseases, mental illnesses present us with the unfortunate necessity of carefully examining the past in order to avoid similar dangers in the future. By "examining the past," I am not even talking about analyzing our childhood but simply looking at what I did yesterday that makes me feel lousy today. We must be detectives, gathering evidence from the clues around us and the trails behind us. We must be weather forecasters, looking ahead for situations that we may need to avoid in order to stay healthy. This can be tedious and tiresome. But that is the nature of chronic illness: it is tedious and tiresome.

Finitude and Loss

Again, I have continued to learn how the restriction of freedom imposed by chronic illness can teach us many painful yet precious lessons. We who live with chronic illnesses and other handicaps are brought up short against our own vulnerability. I have the impression, maybe mistaken, that healthy people can sail right past this contingency until old age hits.

People with chronic illnesses learn earlier than most folks about the preciousness of life. Certainly loss is an ingredient in every human life. But if we allow it to do so, loss can impart wisdom. Facing human limitations and finitude is part of the daily life of the chronically ill. We learn that, contrary to what we might have hoped, human life is delicate, fragile, and transitory. Life-threatening illnesses force us to look into the pit we all will face at one point or another: our own death. Our senses of power, control, freedom, independence—these are misplaced illusions. There is no mastering loss.

I myself am trying to embrace this knowledge of loss of control, or of the hubris of pretense at control, as a gain and privilege. I am succeeding only minimally. I feel that I have been given a second chance. I have had to face my mortality more up close and personal than most people my age. I am a contemporary Ebenezer Scrooge encountering the ghost of Christmas Future. Do I really want to see what that future may hold? Frankly, no. But maybe I, like Ebenezer, will be transformed by God's mercy as I confront my future. Even so, I don't like the nightmare I see.

Recovery?

One of my greatest fears in having written this book is that I may have given false hopes to my readers about "recovery" from mental illnesses. As I have said before, in 2006 I seemed to be doing well. Indeed, I was doing well. But I soon realized that recovery meant something very different from what I had hoped.

In fact, I am not sure I really believe in the concept of "recovery." I do know one person who says that she has recovered from her mental illness. She is symptom-free, off medication, and is no longer under the care of a psychiatrist. I do not share this experience. I myself will never "recover" in this sense. But I do choose every day to make an attempt at reconstruction. Some days are more successful than others.

Even though mental illness has no cure, we can and do make daily choices toward reconstruction. We can choose to take our medication or not. We can choose to continue in psychotherapy or not. We can choose to exercise or sit on the couch. We can choose to eat well or poorly. We can choose to seek out the company of others, or we can isolate ourselves.

And we can choose to avoid situations and people that have been toxic for our health in the past. For example, I have a friend who prefers to spend Thanksgiving and Christmas alone in her own home rather than with her family, who have been so hateful toward her. This is her way of protecting herself from her own symptoms, which recur when she is in the company of her family.

I myself must avoid at all costs images and reports of violence and human pain. This means, of course, that I watch very little TV, and I go to the movies infrequently and, when I do, with trepidation. Reading the newspaper is a risk that I usually choose to take, but I try my best to avoid articles with graphic verbal or photographic depictions of tragedy. I must be ready to turn off the radio, leave the room, or interrupt a conversation immediately to protect myself. This means that I may not always be a very polite conversation partner.

With regard to the concept of reconstruction, I have found very helpful Andrew Solomon's observation in his TED talk that "the opposite of depression is not happiness, but vitality." He is right. People who are depressed are not necessarily sad. They may be sad, but more to the point, they have lost their vitality. And it is this vitality in the first place that gives anyone the energy and courage to work toward reconstruction. When people are profoundly depressed, making the kinds of choices that can promote health is simply not possible. I do not know what recovery would look like at that point.

"Patient" or "Consumer"?

Since the first edition I have also reflected critically on terminology that is current among advocacy groups for the mentally ill. I cannot abide the fashion of replacing the word *patient* with the word *consumer* to speak of those of us who live with mental illnesses. I understand the reasoning behind the choice of the word *consumer* over against *patient*. Promoted by advocacy groups such as NAMI and government agencies such as DMHAS and NIMH, the substitution of terms is a well-intended attempt to undercut the stigma of mental illness. I myself find it counterproductive toward this goal.

Why? I would never "consume" mental health care services if I had any choice in the matter. I do have many choices in life: I "consume" my food; I purchase my car; I buy my computer. But I do not choose to "consume" mental health care. I simply must. I do not freely choose to do so.

Not only does the term "consumer" blur the fact that I have no choice in seeking mental health care, but it is also grounded in capitalist and materialist understandings of what it means to be human in a social context. It betrays an insulting interpretation of what it means to live with a mental illness.

The word *patient*, however, is based on and reinforces the biological model of mental illness more than the term *consumer* does. The biological model is generally assumed to be useful at reducing stigma. I often agree with this assumption.

Patients with biological diseases, among which mental illnesses are counted according to the biological model, may need hospitalization at times. Other hospitalized patients, such as cancer patients and patients with cardiovascular diseases, are not called *consumers*. Like other patients, we who live with mental illnesses may have relatively little choice in the array of treatments we must undergo. Granted, etymology does not determine meaning, but I will point out that the word *patient* is derived from the Latin verb meaning "to suffer, to endure." I don't "consume." I suffer. I would plead for the return of the word *patient*. I myself choke on the word *consumer* and cannot bring myself to say it in reference to people who live with mental illnesses.

"Everyone Is a Little Mentally Ill"

I also reject the suggestion that everyone is a little mentally ill. My guess is that this too is an attempt to undercut stigma: mental illness is not just "out there" but "in here" too. Everyone has it. Another version of this idea is to suggest that there is a continuum or spectrum of mental illness. I believe that it is true that mental illnesses manifest themselves along a continuum of severity of disorders, but this is different from saying everybody lives with a degree of mental illness.

I have heard the phrase "everyone is a little mentally ill" mostly on the lips of family members of patients. My impression is that this idea comforts them. Maybe it helps them think of their loved ones as less stigmatized. If everyone is a little mentally ill, then the son who took a gun to his head and blew out his brains is more "normal" than he might otherwise seem. If everyone is a little mentally ill, the daughter who is disabled by the voices in her head is not really so different from her peers.

I firmly support trying to comfort families. If believing that everyone is a little mentally ill helps them endure witnessing the pain of their loved one, then we should certainly not discourage this belief. And I do see the benefit in encouraging the general public not to "other" those who live with mental illnesses. But I would seek to find another way to do this.

Yes, everyone has annoying faults and foibles, but mental illness is of another order. It is a world apart from "normal" mental function and reality. It is incapacitating in a way that personal foibles, as annoying as they may be, simply are not. Suggesting that everyone is a little mentally ill is demeaning to the experience of those who live with Major Mental Illnesses.

The Biological Model and the Soul

Especially over the last forty years or so the psychiatric guild has come to understand more fully mental illnesses as diseases with biochemical and genetic roots. I personally have found this biological explanatory model to be a double-edged sword.

I do believe that mental illnesses are largely biochemical events. This does not seem counterintuitive: we are human beings inhabiting physical bodies. Of course we are influenced by our biology. Of course mental illnesses are biological phenomena.

I do believe that the biological model for understanding mental illnesses helps to reduce the social stigma and personal sense of shame of having a mental illness. My brain disorder is not my fault any more than my friend's cancer is her fault. Reducing stigma and shame is crucial to the well-being of those who live with the challenges of mental illness, and insofar as the biological model helps, I am all for it.[3]

However, understanding mental illnesses as purely biologically based has the unfortunate potential consequence of pushing aside spiritual questions. It buys into our larger cultural assumptions that all human reality is material. But even psychiatrists who firmly hold to the biological model will insist that biology is not destiny. Mental illnesses are too complex to pinpoint a single cause. The biological model, strictly understood, does not hold water even among psychiatrists and research scientists.

Part of the problem for the church when we focus on the biological model alone is that it gets us off the hook for the spiritual care of mentally ill patients. "They don't really need spiritual care; they just need medication and the hospital." It also can get the Christian patient off the hook from actively seeking spiritual nourishment in the dark times. "I will just take my medication and ignore my spiritual disciplines." If we chalk mental illnesses up to chemical events alone, we may mute the question of how we collude spiritually (and psychologically) in our own illnesses. This is very dangerous.

Christian faith teaches that the human creature is not reducible simply to biological events and functions. Nor are we a little bit biological over here and a little bit spiritual over there. In Scripture, the human creature is body and soul. Both body and soul are created good by God and are blessed in that unity. We are embodied souls, and we are ensouled bodies.

How then do the spiritual and physical relate with respect to our health? Can we honestly say that our spiritual health is on the left and our physical health is on the right? I do not believe this separation is possible. If human creatures are both physical and spiritual in one package, then so is their health. What would this mean for psychiatric care? I do not presume to have immediate answers to this, but I do think psychiatric care would look very different if we took this seriously. So would the church's pastoral care. And as a Christian priest, I am concerned with the latter. It is the central question for the church as we try to care for the bodies and souls of our flock who struggle with mental illnesses.

Our enemies are not only material. They are also spiritual. We struggle with flesh and blood along with powers beyond our creaturely realm. We must pray like the widow pleading to the judge (Luke 18:3) that God will vindicate us against our adversary. We too are in bondage in our own "usurped town," our own Jerusalem under foreign domination. We too are in exile from ourselves and from God. We cry out for freedom, which is a freedom found only in bondage to God. There we will find our true health, our life, and our joy. I quoted from John Donne's "Holy Sonnet 14" in the body of this book, and I close with the full sonnet here.

> Batter my heart, three-person'd God, for you
> yet but knock, breathe, shine, and seek to mend;
> That I may rise and stand, o'erthrow me, and bend
> Your force to break, blow, burn, and make me new.
> I, like an usurp'd town to another due,
> Labor to admit you, but oh, to no end;
> Reason, your viceroy in me, me should defend,
> But is captiv'd, and proves weak or untrue.
> Yet dearly I love you, and would be lov'd fain,
> But am betroth'd unto your enemy;
> Divorce me, untie or break that knot again,
> Take me to you, imprison me, for I,
> Except you enthrall me, never shall be free,
> Nor ever chaste, except you ravish me.
>
> —Lent 2015

Why and How I Use Scripture

Teach me, O LORD, the way of your statutes,
and I shall keep it to the end.

Psalm 119:33

Scripture can be vitally important to the mentally ill Christian. It bears to her not only the voice and will of the triune God but also the community of faith which she cannot often see or feel immediately. Reading Scripture is a discipline that at times in mental illness is almost impossible and yet remains necessary for spiritual health. Why is this so? Because Scripture bears the saving grace of God. It witnesses to the God who loves and elects the unsuspecting Israel, who brings in God's victory over the powers of evil and death in the life, death, and resurrection of Jesus Christ. This backhanded working through history continues throughout Scripture, which is part of the reason that we must read it again and again.

Lord, you have given us your word for a light to shine on our path. Inspire us to meditate on that word, and follow its teaching, that

we may find in it the light which shines more and more until it is
perfect day, through Jesus Christ our Lord. Amen.

Jerome (340–420)

Scripture does not tell a story we naturally know. It tells an
odd story, not one that we would always and everywhere be comfortable with. It tells a story that breaks fresh from the page to
witness again and again to the love of God in Jesus Christ. It
surprises us again and again. This surprise of God is healing to
body, mind, and spirit. And this is why we must read it again and
again, every day, because each time we approach Scripture it will
tell us something new.

I read Scripture because in it I find the Lord of life, the crucified
and risen King who claims victory over all deathly powers. This is
true whether I am mentally healthy or ill. But for someone who is
mentally ill, encountering the Lord of life when all one can think
about is death and despair is not only surprising, indeed shocking,
but also healing. I found this true especially when reading the areas
of the canon that I don't often read in devotions and the Daily
Office, especially the corners and back passageways of the Old
Testament. The Old Testament may seem more difficult for the
Christian to understand than the New Testament. But the struggle
to read the Old Testament reaps great blessing and confers upon
us a new identity, as God gave Jacob a new name after his struggle
at the Jabbok (Gen. 32). The Psalms were also very important
to me, because we read them regularly in the Daily Office. They
speak very meaningfully to the one who suffers.

It is a wondrous and beneficial thing that the Holy Spirit organized
the Holy Scripture so as to satisfy hunger by means of its plainer
passages and remove boredom by means of its obscurer ones.

Augustine (354–430)

But how does one read Scripture? If theologians are trained to
read Scripture at all, we are trained to read it as historical critics.

But reading the Noah cycle and pulling apart the sources is not very edifying to the soul.[1] Questioning whether Jesus really said such and such or whether his statement is from Q or special to Matthew is not very nourishing.[2] As we read Scripture, it is as though these theologically puny questions and their punier answers from much of the so-called higher biblical criticism wring out of us any interest in questions of existence and faithfulness to the God of Jesus Christ.

I follow the standard traditional practice of reading Scripture against itself (*scriptura sui interpres*: Scripture is its own interpreter). This came to be an important practice in the Reformation but can also be seen throughout the history of biblical reading long before then. It is an interpretive practice even within the canon itself. To claim that Scripture is its own interpreter is not to imply that Scripture needs no human interpreter. Of course, the human subject always confronts the Word with her own questions, interests, and presuppositions. And different interpreters come up with different interpretations. This is clear.

But reading Scripture against itself means to acknowledge the theological unity of the canon. I read Matthew and then turn to Isaiah and its voice quoted in Matthew. I read Galatians, then turn to James, without throwing up my hands in despair at the seeming contradictions. The point is not to claim that Matthew misquotes Isaiah or that Galatians cancels out James's voice or vice versa, but that by reading one text against another we learn more. We can dig out the marrow of Scripture by reading it according to itself.

> Blessed Lord, who caused all holy Scriptures to be written for our learning: Grant us so to hear them, read, mark, learn and inwardly digest them, that we may embrace and ever hold fast the blessed hope of everlasting life, which you have given us in our Savior Jesus Christ; who lives and reigns with you and the Holy Spirit, one God, for ever and ever. Amen.
>
> BCP, 236

I read Scripture with the traditional claim that it is inspired of God. When I find a particular "error" or "inconsistency," I question why it may appear as such, what it might tell me about the Divine Voice. I do not take such "errors" to be indicative of a lack of meaning or of Scripture's being "falsified." To say that Scripture is inspired is to say that it has a purpose, it has a direction. It is not to make an argument for Scripture's accuracy or textual perfection, but rather and quite simply to say that Scripture is for us, *pro nobis*. In this it is not like any other text, nor is it read like any other text, although it certainly can be. But when one is at the brink of death, one reads Scripture with a thirst that it will say something hopeful, nourishing, promising, redemptive.

I read Scripture according to the Rule of Faith. In the first through third centuries, both within the canon and among those who commented on it, there were Rules of Faith. These were somewhat like precreedal creeds, based on a trinitarian pattern, and they told the story of Scripture. They were a take on Scripture's whole, the understanding of those who came before orthodoxy but foreshadowed and contributed to it. These Rules were not codified by any churchly council (that came later), and they varied slightly from geographical area to area. Based on Scripture's story, they were reapplied to Scripture in interpretation. They yielded a set or circle of interpretations within which readings were deemed to be faithful and outside of which they were not. In the second century, Irenaeus used the analogy of a mosaic: just as there is a pattern shaped with the tiles of the mosaic that governs the tiles' assembly, so there is a pattern in the Rule of Faith which governs Scripture's interpretation. Irenaeus then uses another illustration: one can use the same tiles to put together a mosaic of the king or, using another pattern, a mosaic of a dog. The Rule of Faith, also known as the Rule of Truth, is the church's "pattern" to render the portrait of the King. In the fifth century, Augustine added another guide which I also try to follow: the Rule of Love. This means that one can legitimately argue for any interpretation of Scripture that does not contradict the faith of the church or the love of God and neighbor. Notice that these rules are proscriptive, not prescriptive rules. They merely disallow interpretations that we *cannot* offer, but they do not dictate the interpretations which we *must* offer. In this regard, the ancient Rules of Faith and Love allow for far more inclusive, flexible, and creative interpretation of Scripture than do most modern historical critical methods.

I read the Old and New Testaments as one canon. That is, I do not say to myself, "That Old Testament is just so barbaric and violent. I won't pay any attention to what it says." The Old Testament bears the hope of Israel just as the New Testament bears the hope of the church. It bears the Word just as much (if not arguably more) than the New Testament. When I come across a difficult passage in the Old Testament, or in the New for that matter, I struggle with it until I can discern some meaning in it. If I still can't, I am willing to leave it alone until I am wiser, should such a day ever come, rather than jettisoning it as though it were less profound than I. I understand those who came before me to be the giants on whose shoulders we now sit. We hope for even better vision than they had, but we don't see further than they apart from them.

> If you cannot yet understand, you should leave the matter for the consideration of those who can; and since Scripture does not abandon you in your infirmity, but with a mother's love accompanies your slower steps, you will make progress. Holy Scripture, indeed, speaks in such a way as to mock the proud readers with its heights, terrify the attentive with its depths, feed great souls with its truth and nourish little ones with sweetness.
>
> Augustine

I read Scripture expecting it to speak afresh today as it spoke yesterday. It is directed not only to those of Israel and the Jesus communities but also to our contemporary context. This is another way in which Scripture is unlike many other historical texts. When I read the Psalms, for example, I read them as speaking to my own situation. They comfort me: "LORD, you have searched me out and known me; you know my sitting down and my rising up. . . . Where can I go then from your Spirit? where can I flee from your presence?" (Ps. 139:1–2, 7). They convict me: "Against you and you alone have I sinned" (Ps. 51:4). They make me sing with joy: "Bless the LORD, O my soul, and all that is within me, bless his holy Name" (Ps. 103:1). They welcome even my angry curses: "Let hot burning coals fall upon them; let them be cast into the mire, never to rise up again" (Ps 140:10).

To allow Scripture to speak afresh today, I have learned from early and medieval biblical interpreters not to be limited to one "sense," one meaning, in the Scriptures. In early and medieval biblical interpretation, one often would read first the literal sense of the passage, then the spiritual senses. These included the tropological (or moral) sense; the allegorical sense; and the anagogical sense, or the eschatological or future sense. The classic illustration (from John Cassian) is as follows: Jerusalem according to the literal sense is a city in the Near East; according to the tropological sense it is the human heart; according to the allegorical sense it is the church; and according to the anagogical sense it is the Heavenly City. This was never a rigid structure for early and medieval exegesis, nor am I suggesting that it should be for us now. But this schema of multiple meanings is a departure from the vision of higher criticism, which should be obvious. Nevertheless I find it quite fruitful, especially when reading the Psalms or any other text of Scripture devotionally. After all, the Psalms can seem bloodthirsty and violent at times. How can one read Psalm 137 or similar psalms devotionally unless by transmuting the Babylonian babies, or the enemies, into something else? So when I read the Psalms, my enemies according to the tropological sense were my mood swings, my brain chemistry, thoughts and feelings that were beyond my control. These were truly my enemies. Many people are repulsed by the warlike imagery of the Old Testament. But most of us have figurative, yet very real, enemies that we need to fight and bring to peace in the embrace of God.

In addition, acknowledging that Scripture speaks on multiple levels at the same time allows us to understand Christ as the speaker of the Psalms. Throughout its history the church has understood Christ to be the speaker of the Psalms. It is he who says, "Pray for the peace of Jerusalem" (Ps. 122:6), and it is he who says, "My God, my God, why have you forsaken me?" (Ps. 22:1; cf. Mark 15:34; Matt. 27:46). It is he who says, "Darkness is my only companion" (Ps. 88:18). It is he who says, "You prepare a table before me in the presence of my enemies" (Ps. 23:5). Reading Scripture on different levels of meaning allows for creative and faithfully rich readings.

I also read Scripture as a daughter of the church. This practice brings us back to the use of the Rule of Faith in one sense: I would never (knowingly) offer an interpretation that could damage the church or the faith of any of its "little ones." This brings us into the community of the present, my parish, my diocese, my communion. Past and present, and not only this, but future also. And this brings us back also to the notion of the senses of Scripture, in its anagogical sense referring to the Heavenly City and the Heavenly Banquet. To read Scripture as a daughter of the church is to offer no interpretation that contradicts or demeans the life of faith. Of course this is tricky. People always have differing opinions as to what demeans the life of faith in the body of Christ.

And this is where community comes in. At different points along the way, I have been part of prayer and Bible study groups, intimate groups in which we studied Scripture together. Ultimately Scripture is meant to be read within the context of the church, the body gathered at worship where it is proclaimed, "This is the Word of the Lord." In smaller study groups members can offer various potential readings of Scripture. The community offers of its own, just as during the Sunday sermon the preacher offers her own.

This is why, in addition to Scripture, I have included in this book prayers and sayings from other Christians throughout the history of the church. Even when I felt that darkness was my only companion, I could gain nourishment and holy friendship from those who came before me. Knowing that they experienced their own sufferings and yet were able to praise God was a great source of strength to me. The community throughout the ages was a source of courage. "Therefore, since we are surrounded by so great a cloud of witnesses, let us also lay aside every weight and the sin which clings so closely, and let us run with perseverance the race that is set before us, looking to Jesus the pioneer and perfecter of our faith" (Heb. 12:1–2).

A Brief Checklist of Symptoms and Resources

Symptoms of Depression

A person has five or more of the following symptoms for two weeks or more, or which interfere with that person's life.[1]

Feeling sad, crying more than usual

Major changes in appetite or sleep patterns

Uncharacteristic irritability, anger

Worries, anxieties

Pessimism, feelings of failure

Loss of energy, libido

Unexplained physical aches and pains

Hopelessness, guilt

Inability to concentrate or make decisions

Inability to carry out personal hygiene (bathing, brushing teeth, etc.)

Lack of enjoyment in things formerly enjoyed

Lack of desire to socialize

Recurring thoughts of death or suicide

Symptoms of Mania

Three or more of the following symptoms for two weeks or more, or which interfere with the person's life.

Increased physical and mental activity and energy

Extreme optimism and self-confidence

Exalted sense of self-importance

Irritability, aggressiveness

Decreased need for sleep

Pressured speech and thoughts

Impulsiveness and reckless behavior (spending money, driving, sex, etc.)

Delusions (thinking things that aren't real or true) and hallucinations (seeing things that others do not)

Symptoms of Schizophrenia

Two or more of the following symptoms present over the course of at least one month.[2]

Delusions

Hallucinations

Disorganized speech

Grossly disorganized behavior, or catatonia

Blunting of personality or affect and blunting of will or drive

(Some of these may also be present in severe depression or mania.)

The following organizations and websites may be of some interest and help as you seek therapy.

Bipolar Disorder
http://bipolar.about.com

Daily Office
When you are too sick to leave the house, you can say the Daily Office "with others" on the web. One resource among many is at www.missionstclare.com.

Depression and Bipolar Support Alliance
800-826-3632
www.DBSAlliance.org

National Alliance on Mental Illness (NAMI)
800-950-6264
www.nami.org
NAMI's ministry to faith communities: FaithNet.org
FaithNet has produced a DVD titled "Mental Illness and Families of Faith: How Congregations Can Respond."

National Institute for Mental Health
www.nimh.nih.org

National Mental Health Association
800-969-6642
www.mentalhealthamerica.net

National Suicide Prevention Lifeline
800-273-8255 (273-TALK)
www.suicidepreventionlifeline.org

Postpartum Support International (in Spanish and English)
800-944-4773
www.postpartum.net

QPR Institute
(Question, Persuade, Refer: Ask a Question, Save a Life)
509-536-5100
www.qprinstitute.com

Suicide.org
1-800-SUICIDE (784-2433)
www.suicide.org

Appendix III

Questions for Group Discussion

Can the kind of suffering a person or family experiences in a mental health crisis be redemptive? Do these personal and familial struggles have anything to do at all with the cross of Christ? See Colossians 1:24.

Is there a spiritual difference between the kinds of suffering in mental illnesses and other kinds of physical illnesses?

Is God present in this specific kind of suffering, and if so, how and where?

What is the role of feelings in the life of prayer and devotion for people in mental health crises vis-à-vis other health crises?

What is the value of prayer for someone who is suffering from mental illness? Does prayer "help"? If so, how?

What spiritual lessons can we as Christians learn from people with mental illnesses, from their presence among us, and from the concrete challenges they may present to us? What blessings can these brothers and sisters in Christ bring us? What lessons can they teach us about being human, about God's love?

What does the pastoral command in Galatians 6:2 ("bear one another's burdens and so fulfill the Law of Christ") mean in the context of mental illnesses?

How does bearing one another's burdens look up close and personal when it comes to mental illnesses? Is this different from pastoral support in cases of less-stigmatized illnesses?

The 1962 version of the Canadian Book of Alternative Services removed parts of psalms that were deemed offensive, especially the angry and violent passages. The present version (1985) has returned them (BAS 701). Is this a positive move, and if so, why? Should the violent and angry expressions be used in pastoral care in cases of mental illnesses? What about in public liturgy?

What is the difference between being concerned and pushy with a person who is having suicidal thoughts? When can or should you break confidences? Can you break confidences but still respect privacy? How?

How do you speak with a person or a family after a suicide attempt? Do you try to talk about God? If so, how?

What do we make of Biblical characters who appear to exhibit symptoms of mental illness?

Why does Jesus "rebuke" demons and cast them out rather than healing the afflicted? He makes a distinction between the person and the evil attacking them. Distinguishing between the patient and the illness, the person and the symptoms, can help fight stigma. Discuss.

I believe that mental illnesses are forms of solitary confinement. Columnist David Brooks has noted that post traumatic stress disorder is a form of moral exile (*New York Times*, 2/17/15). What should be the church's role in helping to heal these psychological maladies?

Notes

Preface to the First Edition

1. Mary Daly, *Beyond God the Father: Toward a Philosophy of Women's Liberation* (Boston: Beacon, 1973), 19.

2. Kathryn Greene-McCreight, *Feminist Reconstructions of Christian Doctrine: Narrative Analysis and Appraisal* (New York: Oxford University Press, 2000), chap. 6.

3. Kay Redfield Jamison, *Touched with Fire: Manic-Depressive Illness and the Artistic Temperament* (New York: Free Press, 1993), appendix A, 261–65.

Introduction

1. See chap. 13 for a fuller explication of the modern mind vis-à-vis ideas of God, in particular for brief theological treatments of the "masters of suspicion," Sigmund Freud, Karl Marx, and Ludwig Feuerbach.

2. Pamela Paul, "The Power to Uplift," *Time*, January 17, 2005, 46.

Chapter 2: Mental Illness

1. Jay Neugeboren, *Transforming Madness: New Lives for People Living with Mental Illness* (New York: William Morrow, 1999), 29.

2. Ibid., 30–31.

3. For more information on therapies, see Stanton L. Jones and Richard E. Butman, *Modern Psychotherapies: A Comprehensive Christian Appraisal* (Downers Grove, IL: InterVarsity, 1991).

4. Andrew Solomon, *The Noonday Demon: An Atlas of Depression* (New York: Scribner, 2001), 114.

5. William Styron, *Darkness Visible: A Memoir of Madness* (New York: Vintage, 1990), 62.

6. Solomon, *Noonday Demon*, 50–51.

7. Ibid., 55.

8. Kay Redfield Jamison, *Touched with Fire: Manic-Depressive Illness and the Artistic Temperament* (New York: Free Press, 1993), 107.

9. Ibid., 116, quoting Edgar Allan Poe, "Eleanora," in *The Fall of the House of Usher and Other Writings* (London: Penguin, 1986), 243.

10. *The Autobiography of a Schizophrenic Girl. The True Story of "Renée"* (New York: Penguin, 1968), 11.

11. Clearly not every case of postpartum depression is as severe as some of the examples I mention. Mothers who experience postpartum symptoms, however, need immediate psychiatric care at the first sign of illness. The "baby blues" are normal in a woman recently having given birth. But when symptoms of depression remain two weeks beyond delivery, help should be sought immediately. Gynecologists and pediatricians are beginning to implement programs of diagnosis at routine visits. Because the mother may not be aware of potential danger, her family will need to be vigilant over what may be possible symptoms and refer her to her gynecologist or the baby's pediatrician.

Chapter 3: Temptation to Suicide

1. Nicholas Wolterstorff, *Lament for a Son* (Grand Rapids: Eerdmans, 1987), 25.

2. For further guidance, see *Preventing Suicide: A Handbook for Pastors, Chaplains and Pastoral Counselors* by Karen Mason (Downers Grove, IL: InterVarsity, 2014).

Chapter 4: Mania

1. Kay Redfield Jamison, *Touched with Fire: Manic-Depressive Illness and the Artistic Temperament* (New York: Free Press, 1993), 249.

Chapter 8: Brain, Mind, and Soul

1. Owen Flanagan, *The Problem of the Soul: Two Visions of Mind and How to Reconcile Them* (New York: Basic Books, 2002), xv. See also Joel B. Green and Stuart Palmer, eds., *In Search of the Soul: Four Views of the Mind-Body Problem* (Downers Grove, IL: InterVarsity, 2005).

2. Richard Swinburne, *The Evolution of the Soul* (Oxford: Clarendon, 1986), 310.

Chapter 9: Sin, Suffering, and Despair

1. This is not to say that the psalmist was "mentally ill," a category that certainly would be only anachronistically applied here. Rather, the mentally ill can identify with the suffering of the psalmist. The psalms of lament all testify to suffering and faithfulness before God.

Chapter 10: Dark Night, Discipline, and the Hiddenness of God

1. John of the Cross, *Dark Night of the Soul* 1.9.3, quoted in Denys Turner, *The Darkness of God* (Cambridge: Cambridge University Press, 1995), 236.

2. Ibid., 243.

3. Elisabeth Sifton, *The Serenity Prayer: Faith and Politics in Times of Peace and War* (New York: Norton, 2003), 7.

Chapter 11: Health and Prayer

1. Larry Dossey, *Healing Words: The Power of Prayer and the Practice of Medicine* (New York: HarperOne, 1993), 248–49.

Chapter 13: Choosing Therapy

1. For example: "Christians who turn from God and His word to psychotherapies for help with depression forsake 'the fountain of living waters' to drink from the polluted and unsatisfying and even harmful 'broken cisterns, that can hold no water' (Jeremiah 13)" (Dave Hunt, *Beyond Seduction* [Eugene, OR: Harvest House, 1987], quoted in Timothy R. Phillips and Mark R. McMinn, introduction to *Care for the Soul: Exploring the Intersection of Psychology and Theology* [Downers Grove, IL: InterVarsity, 2001], 12).

Afterword to the Second Edition

1. E.g., see *Ad Litteram: How Augustine, Calvin and Barth Understand the "Plain Sense" of Genesis 1–3* (New York: Peter Lang, 1999); "Sinews Even in Thy Milk: 13 Observations Regarding Plain Sense Readings of Holy Scripture," *Journal of Theological Interpretation* 2, no. 1 (2007): 19–22; "Introducing Premodern Scriptural Exegesis," *Journal of Theological Interpretation* 4, no. 1 (2010): 1–6.

2. E.g., see *Feminist Reconstructions of Christian Doctrine: Narrative Analysis and Appraisal* (New York: Oxford University Press, 2000); "Feminist Theology and a Generous Orthodoxy," *Scottish Journal of Theology* 57, no. 1 (2004): 95–108; "Feminist Liturgical Trinities and a Generous Orthodoxy," *The Place of Christ in Liturgical Prayer: Trinity, Christology, and Liturgical Theology*, ed. Bryan D. Spinks (Collegeville, MN: Liturgical Press, 2008), 360–78.

3. As for the biological model's potential to reduce stigma, another damaging but well-intended euphemism joins the "patient/consumer" swap. The phrase "behavioral health" has begun to replace the term "mental health." But the term "behavioral health" gives the impression that mental illnesses are caused by and/or result in unacceptable behaviors. How can this help reduce stigma? The use of this term cuts against the biological model's presentation of mental illnesses as chemically and neurologically based bodily diseases. But it is that very model of the root causes of mental illnesses that helps to reduce stigma. An additional problem with the term is the extent to which materialism again plays into the construct of how we present mental illnesses to the public. Health insurance companies trade on the term "behavioral health." By requiring clinicians to assess the patient's behavior, companies can "discern" the effectiveness of treatment they are paying for. This assessment of patient behavior becomes one of the criteria used in health insurance companies' decision of whether to continue or terminate coverage of treatment.

Appendix I: Why and How I Use Scripture

1. The Noah cycle in Gen. 6–9 is apparently composed by two authors, with their material woven together.

2. Q stands for the German *Quelle*, meaning "source." It refers to a hypothetical source of Jesus's sayings that appears in Matthew and Luke but not in Mark.

Appendix II: A Brief Checklist of Symptoms and Resources

1. The first two sets of symptoms in this checklist have been adapted from material put out by the Depression and Bipolar Support Alliance.

2. See also J. Raymond DePaulo and Leslie Alan Horvitz DePaulo, *Understanding Depression: What We Know and What You Can Do about It* (New York: John Wiley & Sons, 2002), 55.

Bibliography

Aamodt, Sandra, and Sam Wang. *Welcome to Your Brain: The Science of Jet Lag, Love and Other Curiosities of Life*. London: Rider, 2008.

———. *Welcome to Your Brain: Why You Lose Your Car Keys but Never Forget How to Drive and Other Puzzles of Everyday Life*. New York: Bloomsbury, 2008.

———. *Welcome to Your Child's Brain: How the Mind Grows from Conception to College*. New York: Bloomsbury, 2011.

Albers, Robert H., William H. Meller. *Ministry with Persons with Mental Illness and Their Families*. Minneapolis: Fortress, 2012.

American Psychiatric Association. *Diagnostic and Statistical Manual of Mental Disorders*. 5th ed. Arlington, VA: American Psychiatric Association, 2013.

Andreasen, Nancy C. *The Broken Brain: The Biological Revolution in Psychiatry*. New York: Harper & Row, 1984.

Aquinas, St. Thomas. *Treatise on Happiness*. Translated by John A. Oesterle. Englewood Cliffs, NJ: Prentice-Hall, 1964.

Arieti, Silvano. *Interpretation of Schizophrenia*. 2nd ed. New York: Basic, 1974.

Asquith, Glenn H., ed. "Vision from a Little Known Country: A Boisen Reader." Decatur, GA: Journal of Pastoral Care Publications, 1991.

Baechler, Jean. *Suicides*. Translated by Barry Cooper. New York: Basic, 1979.

Balmary, Marie. *Psychoanalyzing Psychoanalysis: Freud and the Hidden Fault of the Father*. Translated by Ned Lukacher. Baltimore: Johns Hopkins University Press, 1982.

Bauby, Jean-Dominique. *The Diving Bell and the Butterfly*. Translated by Jeremy Leggatt. New York: Knopf, 1997.

Baxter, William E., and David W. Hathcox III. *America's Care of the Mentally Ill: A Photographic History*. Washington, DC: American Psychiatric Press, 1994.

Beers, Clifford Whittingham. *A Mind That Found Itself: An Autobiography.* New York: Doubleday, 1937.

Bernstein, Judith R. *When the Bough Breaks: Forever after the Death of a Son or Daughter.* Kansas City, MO: Andrews and McMeel, 1997.

Birkhead, L. M., ed. *From Sin to Psychiatry: An Interview on the Way to Mental Health with Dr. Karl A. Menninger.* Girard, KS: Haldeman-Julius, 1931.

Blatt, Sidney J. *Experiences of Depression: Theoretical, Clinical, and Research Perspectives.* Washington, DC: American Psychological Association, 2004.

Blueler, Manfred. *The Schizophrenic Disorders: Long-Term Parent and Family Studies.* Translated by Siegfried M. Clemens. New Haven: Yale University Press, 1978.

Boisen, Anton T., ed. *The Exploration of the Inner World: A Study of Mental Disorder and Religious Experience.* New York: Harper, 1962.

———. *Lift Up Your Hearts: A Service Book for Use in Hospitals.* Boston: Pilgrim, 1926.

———. *Out of the Depths: An Autobiographical Study of Mental Disorder and Religious Experience.* New York: Harper, 1960.

———. *Religion in Crisis and Custom: A Sociological and Psychological Study.* New York: Harper, 1955.

Bonanno, George A. *The Other Side of Sadness: What the New Science of Bereavement Tells Us about Life after Loss.* New York: Basic, 2009.

Bonhoeffer, Dietrich. *Spiritual Care.* Translated by Jay C. Rochelle. Philadelphia: Fortress, 1985.

Bowlby, John. *Attachment.* Vol. 1 of *Attachment and Loss.* 2d ed. New York: Basic, 1982.

———. *Sadness and Depression.* Vol. 3 of *Attachment and Loss.* New York: Basic, 1980.

———. *Separation: Anxiety and Anger.* Vol. 2 of *Attachment and Loss.* New York: Basic, 1973.

Boyd, Jeffrey H. *Being Sick Well: Joyful Living Despite Chronic Illness.* Grand Rapids: Baker Books, 2005.

Brinks, Herbert J. *Pine Rest Christian Hospital, 75 Years: 1910–1985.* Cutlerville, MI: Pine Rest Christian Hospital, 1985.

Brown, Warren S., Nancey Murphy, and H. Newton Malony, eds. *Whatever Happened to the Soul?: Scientific and Theological Portraits of Human Nature.* Minneapolis: Fortress, 1998.

Burton, Robert. *The Anatomy of Melancholy.* Edited by Floyd Dell and Paul Jordan-Smith. New York: George H. Doran, 1927.

Bush, Michael D., ed. *This Incomplete One: Words Occasioned by the Death of a Young Person.* Grand Rapids: Eerdmans, 2006.

Byassee, Jason. *Praise Seeking Understanding: Reading the Psalms with Augustine.* Grand Rapids: Eerdmans, 2007.

Calvin, John. *Institutes of the Christian Religion.* Edited by John T. McNeill. Translated by Ford Lewis Battles. Philadelphia: Westminster, 1960.

Casey, Nell, ed. *Unholy Ghost: Writers on Depression.* New York: Harper Perennial, 2002.

Charry, Ellen T. *God and the Art of Happiness.* Grand Rapids: Eerdmans, 2010.

Chase-Ziolek, Mary. *Health, Healing, and Wholeness: Engaging Congregations in Ministries of Health.* Cleveland: Pilgrim, 2005.

Cheney, Terri. *Manic: A Memoir.* New York: William Morrow, 2008.

Choron, Jacques. *Death and Western Thought.* New York: Collier, 1973.

Clebsch, William A., and Charles R. Jaekle. *Pastoral Care in Historical Perspective.* New York: Harper & Row, 1967.

Clinebell, Howard J., Jr. *Mental Health through Christian Community: The Local Church's Ministry of Growth and Healing.* New York: Abingdon, 1965.

Cockburn, Patrick, and Henry Cockburn. *Henry's Demons: Living with Schizophrenia: A Father and Son's Story.* New York: Scribner, 2011.

Cole, Allan Hugh. *Be Not Anxious: Pastoral Care of Disquieted Souls.* Grand Rapids: Eerdmans, 2008.

Colwell, John E. *Why Have You Forsaken Me? A Personal Reflection on the Experience of Desolation.* Eugene, OR: Cascade, 2012.

Corbett, Lionel. *The Sacred Cauldron: Psychotherapy as a Spiritual Practice.* Wilmette, IL: Chiron Publications, 2011.

Cozolino, Louis. *The Healthy Aging Brain: Sustaining Attachment, Attaining Wisdom.* New York: Norton, 2008.

———. *The Neuroscience of Psychotherapy: Building and Rebuilding the Human Brain.* New York: Norton, 2002.

Crafton, Barbara Cawthorne. *Jesus Wept: When Faith and Depression Meet.* San Francisco: Jossey-Bass, 2009.

Cronkite, Kathy. *On the Edge of Darkness: Conversations about Conquering Depression.* New York: Doubleday, 1994.

Dain, Norman. *Concepts of Insanity in the United States, 1789–1865.* New Brunswick, NJ: Rutgers University Press, 1964.

Dale, Ryan, and Juanita Dale. *Rooted in God's Love: Biblical Meditations for People in Recovery.* Downers Grove, IL: InterVarsity, 1992.

Davidson, Charles. *Bone Dead and Rising: Vincent Van Gogh and the Self Before God.* Eugene, OR: Cascade, 2011.

Davidson, Richard J., and Sharon Begley. *The Emotional Life of Your Brain: How Its Unique Patterns Affect the Way You Think, Feel, and Live—and How You Can Change Them.* New York: Hudson Street, 2012.

Dawn, Marva J. *Being Well When We're Ill: Wholeness and Hope in Spite of Infirmity.* Minneapolis: Augsburg, 2008.

de Beausobre, Iulia. *Creative Suffering.* London: Dacre, 1946.

de Caussade, J.-P. *Abandonment to Divine Providence.* Edited by J. Ramière. Translated by E. J. Strickland. San Francisco: Ignatius, 2011.

DePaulo, J. Raymond, and Leslie Ann Horwitz. *Understanding Depression: What We Know and What You Can Do about It.* New York: Wiley, 2002.

Deutsch, Albert. *The Mentally Ill in America: A History of Their Care and Treatment from Colonial Times*. Garden City, NY: Doubleday, 1937.

de Young, Mary. *Madness: An American History of Mental Illness and Its Treatment*. Jefferson, NC: McFarland, 2010.

Donne, John. *Biathanatos. A Declaration of That Paradoxe, or Thesis, That Selfe-Homicide Is not So Naturally Sinne, That It May Never Be Otherwise*. London: J. Dawson, 1644.

————. *Devotions upon Emergent Occasions*. Edited by John Sparrow. Philadelphia: R. West, 1978.

————. *Religious Poetry and Prose*. Edited by Henry L. Carrigan. Brewster, MA: Paraclete, 1999.

Donnelly, Michael. *Managing the Mind: A Study of Medical Psychology in Early Nineteenth-Century Britain*. London: Tavistock, 1983.

Dossey, Larry. *Healing Words: The Power of Prayer and the Practice of Medicine*. San Francisco: HarperOne, 1993.

————. *Meaning and Medicine: Lessons from a Doctor's Tales of Breakthrough and Healing*. New York: Bantam, 1991.

————. *Prayer Is Good Medicine: How to Reap the Healing Benefits of Prayer*. San Francisco: HarperOne, 1996.

Dunlap, Susan J. *Counseling Depressed Women*. Louisville: Westminster John Knox, 1997.

Durkheim, Émile. *Suicide: A Study in Sociology*. Edited by George Simpson. Translated by John A. Spaulding and George Simpson. New York: Free Press, 1966.

Earley, Pete. *Crazy: A Father's Search through America's Mental Health Madness*. New York: Putnam, 2006.

Evans, Abigail Rian. *Is God Still at the Bedside? The Medical, Ethical, and Pastoral Issues of Death and Dying*. Grand Rapids: Eerdmans, 2011.

Fast, Julia A., and John D. Preston. *Loving Someone with Bipolar Disorder: Understanding and Helping Your Partner*. Oakland, CA: New Harbinger, 2004.

Fawcett, Jan, Bernard Golden, and Nancy Rosenfeld. *New Hope for People with Bipolar Disorder*. Roseville, CA: Prima, 2000.

Fehrenbach, Paul K. *Soul and Self: Parallels between Spiritual and Psychological Growth*. New York: Paulist Press, 2006.

Fink, Max. *Electroconvulsive Therapy: A Guide for Professionals and Their Patients*. New York: Oxford University Press, 2010.

Fink, Paul Jay, and Allan Tasman, eds. *Stigma and Mental Illness*. Washington, DC: American Psychiatric Press, 1992.

Flach, Frederic F. *The Secret Strength of Depression*. Philadelphia: Lippincott, 1974.

Flanagan, Owen. *The Problem of the Soul: Two Visions of Mind and How to Reconcile Them*. New York: Basic, 2002.

Ford, David. *The Shape of Living: Spiritual Directions for Everyday Life*. Grand Rapids: Baker Books, 1997.

Foucault, Michel. *History of Madness*. Translated by Jonathan Murphy and Jean Khalfa. London: Routledge, 2009.

———. *Madness and Civilization: A History of Insanity in the Age of Reason.* Translated by Richard Howard. New York: Vintage, 1988.

Fran, Renee. *What Happened to Mommy?* New York: Eastman, 1994.

Fromm, Erich. *Psychoanalysis and Religion.* New Haven: Yale University Press, 1959.

Gamwell, Lynn, and Nancy Tomes. *Madness in America: Cultural and Medical Perceptions of Mental Illness before 1914.* Ithaca, NY: Cornell University Press, 1995.

Garrett, Greg. *Crossing Myself: A Story of Spiritual Rebirth.* Colorado Springs: NavPress, 2006.

Gibbons, Kaye. *Sights Unseen.* New York: Putnam, 1995.

Goffman, Erving. *Asylums: Essays on the Social Situation of Mental Patients and Other Inmates.* New York: Doubleday, 1961.

———. *Stigma: Notes on the Management of Spoiled Identity.* New York: Simon & Schuster, 1986.

Govig, Stewart D. *Souls Are Made of Endurance: Surviving Mental Illness in the Family.* Louisville: Westminster John Knox, 1994.

———. *Strong at the Broken Places: Persons with Disabilities and the Church.* Louisville: Westminster John Knox, 1989.

Granello, Darcy Haag, and Paul F. Granello. *Suicide: An Essential Guide for Helping Professionals and Educators.* Boston: Pearson, 2007.

Green, Joel, ed. *What about the Soul? Neuroscience and Christian Anthropology.* Nashville: Abingdon, 2004.

Green, Joel B., and Stuart L. Palmer, eds. *In Search of the Soul: Four Views of the Mind-Body Problem.* Downers Grove, IL: InterVarsity, 2005.

Gregg-Schroeder, Susan. *In the Shadow of God's Wings: Grace in the Midst of Depression.* Nashville: Upper Room, 1998.

Greider, Kathleen J. *Much Madness Is Divinest Sense: Wisdom in Memoirs of Soul-Suffering.* Cleveland: Pilgrim, 2007.

Griffith, James L., and Melissa Elliott Griffith. *Encountering the Sacred in Psychotherapy: How to Talk with People about Their Spiritual Lives.* New York: Guilford, 2002.

Grob, Gerald N. *From Asylum to Community: Mental Health Policy in Modern America.* Princeton: Princeton University Press, 1991.

———. *The Mad among Us: A History of the Care of America's Mentally Ill.* New York: Free Press, 1994.

———. *Mental Illness and American Society, 1875–1940.* Princeton: Princeton University Press, 1983.

Groopman, Jerome. *The Anatomy of Hope: How People Prevail in the Face of Illness.* New York: Random House, 2004.

Guthrie, Nancy, ed. *Be Still, My Soul: Embracing God's Purpose and Provision in Suffering: 25 Classic and Contemporary Readings on the Problem of Pain.* Wheaton: Crossway, 2010.

Hall, Douglas John. *God and Human Suffering: An Exercise in the Theology of the Cross.* Minneapolis: Augsburg, 1986.

Harley, David. *By Faith and Failure: When God Takes Hold of Right Steps and Wrong Turns*. Singapore: Zoie, 2007.

Hauerwas, Stanley. *Naming the Silences: God, Medicine, and the Problem of Suffering*. Grand Rapids: Eerdmans, 1990.

Healy, David. *Mania: A Short History of Bipolar Disorder*. Baltimore: Johns Hopkins University Press, 2008.

Hecht, Jennifer Michael. *Stay: A History of Suicide and the Philosophies against It*. New Haven: Yale University Press, 2013.

Heckler, Richard A. *Waking Up, Alive: The Descent, the Suicide Attempt, and the Return to Life*. New York: Ballantine, 1994.

Hersh, Julie K. *Struck by Living: From Depression to Hope*. Dallas: Brown Books, 2010.

Holberg, Jennifer L., ed. *Shouts and Whispers: Twenty-One Writers Speak about Their Writing and Their Faith*. Grand Rapids: Eerdmans, 2006.

Holifield, E. Brooks. *A History of Pastoral Care in America: From Salvation to Self-Realization*. Nashville: Abingdon, 1983.

Hornbacher, Marya. *Madness: A Bipolar Life*. London: Fourth Estate, 2008.

Horwitz, Allan V., and Jerome C. Wakefield. *The Loss of Sadness: How Psychiatry Transformed Normal Sorrow into Depressive Disorder*. New York: Oxford University Press, 2007.

Hsu, Albert Y. *Grieving a Suicide: A Loved One's Search for Comfort, Answers and Hope*. Downers Grove, IL: InterVarsity, 2002.

Hunsinger, Deborah van Deusen. *Pray without Ceasing: Revitalizing Pastoral Care*. Grand Rapids: Eerdmans, 2006.

———. *Theology and Pastoral Counseling: A New Interdisciplinary Approach*. Grand Rapids: Eerdmans, 1995.

Hurley, Daniel. *Facing Pain, Finding Hope: A Physician Examines Pain, Faith, and the Healing Stories of Jesus*. Chicago: Loyola, 2005.

Ilardi, Stephen S. *The Depression Cure: The 6-Step Program to Beat Depression without Drugs*. Cambridge, MA: Da Capo, 2009.

James, William. *The Varieties of Religious Experience: A Study in Human Nature*. New York: Collier, 1961.

Jamison, Kay Redfield. *Night Falls Fast: Understanding Suicide*. New York: Knopf, 1999.

———. *Touched with Fire: Manic-Depressive Illness and the Artistic Temperament*. New York: Free Press, 1993.

———. *An Unquiet Mind: A Memoir of Moods and Madness*. New York: Knopf, 1995.

Jimenez, Mary Ann. *Changing Faces of Madness: Early American Attitudes and Treatment of the Insane*. Hanover, NH: Brandeis University Press, 1987.

Jones, Stanton L., and Richard E. Butman. *Modern Psychotherapies: A Comprehensive Christian Appraisal*. Downers Grove, IL: InterVarsity, 1991.

Karp, David A. *The Burden of Sympathy: How Families Cope with Mental Illness*. New York: Oxford University Press, 2001.

————. *Speaking of Sadness: Depression, Disconnection, and the Meaning of Illness*. New York: Oxford University Press, 1996.

Kaysen, Susanna. *Girl, Interrupted*. New York: Turtle Bay, 1993.

Keck, Beverly Buller. *Just One More Day: Meditations for Those Who Struggle with Anxiety and Depression*. Winnipeg, MB: Kindred Productions, 2009.

Keck, David. *Forgetting Whose We Are: Alzheimer's Disease and the Love of God*. Nashville: Abingdon, 1996.

Kehoe, Nancy. *Wrestling with Our Inner Angels: Faith, Mental Illness, and the Journey to Wholeness*. San Francisco: Jossey-Bass, 2009.

Kierkegaard, Søren. *The Concept of Anxiety*. Translated by Reidar Thomte. Princeton: Princeton University Press, 1980.

————. *The Sickness unto Death: A Christian Psychological Exposition for Upbuilding and Awakening*. Translated by Howard V. Hong and Edna H. Hong. Princeton: Princeton University Press, 1980.

Koenig, Harold G. *Faith and Mental Health: Religious Resources for Healing*. Philadelphia: Templeton Foundation, 2005.

Komarek, Paul, and Andrea Schroer. *Defying Mental Illness: Finding Recovery with Community Resources and Family Support*. Cincinnati: Church Basement Press, 2011.

Kübler-Ross, Elisabeth, ed. *Death: The Final Stage of Growth*. Englewood Cliffs, NJ: Prentice-Hall, 1975.

Kushner, Harold S. *When Bad Things Happen to Good People*. New York: Schocken, 1981.

Laing, R. D. *The Divided Self: An Existential Study in Sanity and Madness*. Harmondsworth, UK: Penguin, 1965.

Law, William. *A Serious Call to a Devout and Holy Life*. Grand Rapids: Eerdmans, 1966.

Leithart, Peter J. *Gratitude: An Intellectual History*. Waco: Baylor University Press, 2014.

Lethbridge, Lucy, and Selina O'Grady, eds. *A Deep but Dazzling Darkness: An Anthology of Personal Experiences of God*. London: Darton, Longman & Todd, 2002.

Lewis, C. S. *The Problem of Pain*. London: Collins, 1982.

Long, Thomas G. *What Shall We Say? Evil, Suffering, and the Crisis of Faith*. Grand Rapids: Eerdmans, 2011.

Lowenthal, David. *The Past Is a Foreign Country*. Cambridge: Cambridge University Press, 1985.

Malania, Leo, ed. *Ministry to the Sick: According to the Use of the Episcopal Church as Set Forth in the Book of Common Prayer*. New York: Church Publishing, 1998.

Marsh, Diane T., and Rex Dickens. *How to Cope with Mental Illness in Your Family: A Self-Care Guide for Siblings, Offspring, and Parents*. New York: Penguin, 1997.

Martyn, Dorothy W. *Beyond Deserving: Children, Parents, and Responsibility Revisited*. Grand Rapids: Eerdmans, 2007.

————. *The Man in the Yellow Hat: Theology and Psychoanalysis in Child Therapy*. Atlanta: Scholars Press, 1992.

Mason, Karen. *Preventing Suicide: A Handbook for Pastors, Chaplains, and Pastoral Counselors.* Downers Grove, IL: InterVarsity, 2014.

Mays, John Bentley. *In the Jaws of the Black Dogs: A Memoir of Depression.* London: Viking, 1995.

McMinn, Mark R., and Timothy R. Phillips, ed. *Care for the Soul: Exploring the Intersection of Psychology and Theology.* Downers Grove, IL: InterVarsity, 2001.

McNeill, John T. *A History of the Cure of Souls.* New York: Harper & Row, 1951.

Miklowitz, David Jay. *Bipolar Disorder: A Family-Focused Treatment Approach.* New York: Guilford, 2008.

"Ministering in Crisis." *Contact: The Ministry Magazine of Gordon Conwell Theological Seminary* 36, no. 2 (2007).

Moller, Mary D. "Meeting Spiritual Needs on an Inpatient Unit." *Journal of Psychosocial Nursing and Mental Health Services* 37, no. 11 (1999): 5–10.

Mondimore, Francis Mark. *Bipolar Disorder: A Guide for Patients and Families.* Baltimore: Johns Hopkins University Press, 1999.

Moore, Thomas. *Care of the Soul: A Guide for Cultivating Depth and Sacredness in Everyday Life.* New York: HarperCollins, 1992.

Morgan, Robert J. *Then Sings My Soul: 150 of the World's Greatest Hymn Stories.* Nashville: Thomas Nelson, 2003.

Morse, Louise. *Worshipping with Dementia: Meditations, Scriptures and Prayers for Sufferers and Carers.* Oxford: Monarch, 2010.

Morse, Louise, and Robert Hitchings. *Could It Be Dementia? Losing Your Mind Doesn't Mean Losing Your Soul.* Grand Rapids: Monarch, 2008.

Mottram, Kenneth P. *Caring for Those in Crisis: Facing Ethical Dilemmas with Patients and Families.* Grand Rapids: Brazos, 2007.

Nathiel, Susan. *Daughters of Madness: Growing Up and Older with a Mentally Ill Mother.* Westport, CT: Praeger, 2007.

Neugeboren, Jay. *Transforming Madness: New Lives for People Living with Mental Illness.* New York: William Morrow, 1999.

O'Connor, Richard. *Undoing Depression: What Therapy Doesn't Teach You and Medication Can't Give You.* New York: Little, Brown, 2010.

Papolos, Demitri F., and Janice Papolos. *The Bipolar Child: The Definitive and Reassuring Guide to Childhood's Most Misunderstood Disorder.* New York: Broadway, 2002.

Pargament, Kenneth I., and Jeremy Cummings. "Anchored by Faith: Religion as a Resilience Factor." In *Handbook of Adult Resilience,* ed. John W. Riech and Alex J. Zaustra. New York: Guilford, 2010.

Paul, Pamela. "The Power to Uplift." *Time,* January 17, 2005, 46–48.

Plath, Sylvia. *The Bell Jar.* New York: HarperCollins, 1996.

Polkinghorne, John. *The God of Hope and the End of the World.* New Haven: Yale University Press, 2003.

Porter, Roy. *Madness: A Brief History.* New York: Oxford University Press, 2002.

Probst, R. *Psychotherapy in a Religious Framework: Spirituality in the Emotional Healing Process.* New York: Human Sciences Press, 1988.

Rahner, Karl. *On the Theology of Death*. Translated by Charles H. Henkey. New York: Herder & Herder, 1961.

Ramachandran, V. S. *The Tell-Tale Brain: A Neuroscientist's Quest for What Makes Us Human*. New York: Norton, 2011.

Ratey, John J., and Catherine Johnson. *Shadow Syndromes*. London: Bantam, 1997.

Reich, John W., Alex J. Zautra, and John Stuart Hall, eds. *Handbook of Adult Resilience*. New York: Guilford, 2010.

Reiss, Benjamin. *Theaters of Madness: Insane Asylums and Nineteenth-Century American Culture*. Chicago: University of Chicago Press, 2008.

Renée. *Autobiography of a Schizophrenic Girl*. Translated by Grace Rubin-Rabson. New York: New American Library, 1970.

Rittgers, Ronald K. "Martin Luther and the 'Christian Art of Suffering.'" Unpublished paper, 2004.

Rogers, Carl R. *On Becoming a Person: A Therapist's View of Psychotherapy*. Boston: Houghton Mifflin, 1961.

Rosen, George. *Madness in Society: Chapters in the Historical Sociology of Mental Illness*. New York: Harper & Row, 1969.

Rosenzweig, Franz. *Understanding the Sick and the Healthy: A View of World, Man, and God*. Translated by Nahum Glatzer. New York: Noonday, 1999.

Rosner, Brian S. *The Consolations of Theology*. Grand Rapids: Eerdmans, 2008.

Roukema, Richard W. *Counseling for the Soul in Distress: What Every Religious Counselor Should Know about Emotional and Mental Illness*. New York: Haworth, 2003.

Ruether, Rosemary Radford, and David Ruether. *Many Forms of Madness: A Family's Struggle with Mental Illness and the Mental Health System*. Minneapolis: Fortress, 2010.

Sacks, Oliver. *An Anthropologist on Mars: Seven Paradoxical Tales*. New York: Knopf, 1995.

———. *The Man Who Mistook His Wife for a Hat*. New York: Summit, 1985.

Saks, Elyn R. *The Center Cannot Hold: My Journey Through Madness*. New York: Hyperion, 2007.

Salter, Andrew. *The Case against Psychoanalysis*. New York: Harper & Row, 1972.

Scharfetter, Christian. *General Psychopathology: An Introduction*. Translated by Helen Marshall. Cambridge, UK: Cambridge University Press, 1980.

Schiller, Lori, and Amanda Bennett. *The Quiet Room: A Journey Out of the Torment of Madness*. New York: Warner, 1996.

Schioldann-Nielsen, Johan. *Famous and Very Important Persons: Medical, Psychological, Psychiatric Bibliography, 1960–1984*. Odense: Odense University Press, 1986.

Schmidt, Richard H., ed. *Comfort Ye: Finding Light in Times of Darkness*. Cincinnati: Forward Movement, 2007.

Schneidman, Edwin S. *The Suicidal Mind*. Oxford: Oxford University Press, 1996.

Searle, John R. *The Rediscovery of the Mind*. Cambridge, MA: MIT Press, 1992.

Shannonhouse, Rebecca, ed. *Out of Her Mind: Women Writing on Madness*. New York: Modern Library, 2003.

Shorter, Edward. *A History of Psychiatry: From the Era of the Asylum to the Age of Prozac*. New York: Wiley, 1997.

Shults, F. LeRon, and Steven J. Sandage. *Transforming Spirituality: Integrating Theology and Psychology*. Grand Rapids: Baker Academic, 2006.

Siegler, Miriam, and Humphrey Osmond. *Models of Madness, Models of Medicine*. New York: Harper & Row, 1976.

Sifton, Elizabeth. *The Serenity Prayer: Faith and Politics in Times of Peace and War*. New York: Norton, 2003.

Simon, Bennett. *Mind and Madness in Ancient Greece: The Classical Roots of Modern Psychiatry*. Ithaca, NY: Cornell University Press, 1978.

Simpson, Amy. *Anxious: Choosing Faith in a World of Worry*. Downers Grove, IL: InterVarsity, 2014.

———. *Troubled Minds: Mental Illness and the Church's Mission*. Downer's Grove, IL: InterVarsity, 2013.

Sittser, Jerry. *A Grace Disguised: How the Soul Grows through Loss*. Grand Rapids: Zondervan, 2004.

Skoglund, Elizabeth. *More Than Coping: God's Servants Can Triumph over Emotional Pain*. Minneapolis: World Wide Publications, 1979.

Solomon, Andrew. *The Noonday Demon: An Atlas of Depression*. New York: Scribner, 2001.

Southwick, Steven M., and Dennis S. Charney. *Resilience: The Science of Mastering Life's Greatest Challenges*. New York: Cambridge University Press, 2012.

Stackhouse, John G., Jr. *Can God Be Trusted? Faith and the Challenge of Evil*. New York: Oxford University Press, 1998.

Stanford, Matthew S. *Grace for the Afflicted: Viewing Mental Illness through the Eyes of Faith*. Colorado Springs: Paternoster, 2008.

St. John of the Cross. *Dark Night of the Soul: A Classic in the Literature of Mysticism*. New York: Doubleday, 1990.

Stone, Howard W. *Depression and Hope: New Insights for Pastoral Counseling*. Minneapolis: Fortress, 1998.

St. Teresa of Avila. *The Interior Castle*. Translated by E. Alison Peers. New York: Doubleday, 1961.

Styron, William. *Darkness Visible: A Memoir of Madness*. New York: Modern Library, 2007.

Surin, Kenneth. *Theology and the Problem of Evil*. Oxford: Blackwell, 1986.

Swenson, Kristin M. *Living through Pain: Psalms and the Search for Wholeness*. Waco: Baylor University Press, 2005.

Swinburne, Richard. *The Evolution of the Soul*. New York: Oxford University Press, 1986.

Swinton, John. *From Bedlam to Shalom: Towards a Practical Theology of Human Nature, Interpersonal Relationships, and Mental Health Care*. New York: Lang, 2000.

———. *Raging with Compassion: Pastoral Responses to the Problem of Evil*. Grand Rapids: Eerdmans, 2007.

————. *Resurrecting the Person: Friendship and the Care of People with Mental Health Problems.* Nashville: Abingdon, 2000.

Szasz, Thomas S. *The Age of Madness: The History of Involuntary Mental Hospitalization Presented in Selected Texts.* New York: Doubleday, 1973.

Taylor, Jeremy. *The Whole Works of the Right Rev. Jeremy Taylor.* Vol. 3, *The Rule and Exercises of Holy Living and Holy Dying.* London, 1651.

Taylor, Jill Bolte. *My Stroke of Insight: A Brain Scientist's Personal Journey.* New York: Viking, 2008.

Thiel, John E. *God, Evil, and Innocent Suffering: A Theological Reflection.* New York: Crossroad, 2002.

Thielicke, Helmut. *Death and Life.* Translated by Edward H. Schroeder. Philadelphia: Fortress, 1970.

————. *The Silence of God.* Translated by G. W. Bromiley. Grand Rapids: Eerdmans, 1962.

Thiemann, Ronald F., and William C. Placher, eds. *Why Are We Here? Everyday Questions and the Christian Life.* Harrisburg, PA: Trinity Press International, 1998.

Thompson, Tracy. *The Ghost in the House: Motherhood, Raising Children, and Struggling with Depression.* London: Piatkus, 2006.

Tileston, Mary Wilder. *Great Souls at Prayer: Fourteen Centuries of Prayer, Praise and Aspiration, from St. Augustine to Christina Rossetti and Robert Louis Stevenson.* Berkeley: University of California Libraries, 1898.

Torrey, E. Fuller, and Michael B. Knable. *Surviving Manic Depression: A Manual on Bipolar Disorder for Patients, Families, and Providers.* New York: Basic, 2002.

Townsend, Loren L. *Suicide: Pastoral Responses.* Edited by Daniel G. Bagby. Nashville: Abingdon, 2006.

Trimble, Michael R. *The Soul in the Brain: The Cerebral Basis of Language, Art, and Belief.* Baltimore: Johns Hopkins University Press, 2007.

Van Dijk, Sheri. *The Dialectical Behavior Therapy Skills Workbook for Bipolar Disorder: Using DBT to Regain Control of Your Emotions and Your Life.* Oakland, CA: New Harbinger, 2009.

Verhey, Allen. *The Christian Art of Dying: Learning from Jesus.* Grand Rapids: Eerdmans, 2011.

von Speyr, Adrienne. *Lumina and New Lumina.* San Francisco: Ignatius, 2008.

Wagner, Pamela Spiro, and Carolyn S. Spiro. *Divided Minds: Twin Sisters and Their Journey through Schizophrenia.* New York: St. Martin's Press, 2005.

Wahl, Otto F. *Telling Is Risky Business. Mental Health Consumers Confront Stigma.* New Brunswick, NJ: Rutgers University Press, 1999.

Warnock, Mary. *Memory.* London: Faber & Faber, 1987.

Waterhouse, Steven. *Strength for His People: A Ministry for Families of the Mentally Ill.* Amarillo, TX: Westcliff, 2002.

Watson, J. R., ed. *An Annotated Anthology of Hymns.* New York: Oxford University Press, 2002.

Webber, Christopher L., ed. *Give Us Grace: An Anthology of Anglican Prayers.* Harrisburg, PA: Morehouse, 2004.

Wiesel, Elie. *Night.* Translated by Stella Rodway. New York: Bantam, 1982.

Williams, Mark, et al. *The Mindful Way through Depression: Freeing Yourself from Chronic Unhappiness.* New York: Guilford, 2007.

Winerip, Michael. *9 Highland Road.* New York: Pantheon, 1994.

Wolterstorff, Nicholas. *Lament for a Son.* Grand Rapids: Eerdmans, 1987.

Worthington, Everett L., ed. *Psychotherapy and Religious Values.* Grand Rapids: Baker, 1993.

Yalom, Irvin D. *The Gift of Therapy: An Open Letter to a New Generation of Therapists and Their Patients.* New York: HarperCollins, 2002.

————. *Momma and the Meaning of Life: Tales of Psychotherapy.* New York: Perennial, 2000.

————. *The Theory and Practice of Group Psychotherapy.* 2nd ed. New York: Basic, 1975.

Yarhouse, Mark A., Richard E. Butman, and Barrett W. McRay. *Modern Psychopathologies: A Comprehensive Christian Appraisal.* Downers Grove, IL: InterVarsity, 2005.

Yong, Amos. *The Bible, Disability, and the Church: A New Vision of the People of God.* Grand Rapids: Eerdmans, 2011.

————. *Hospitality and the Other: Pentecost, Christian Practices, and the Neighbor.* Maryknoll, NY: Orbis, 2008.

————. *Theology and Down Syndrome: Reimagining Disability in Late Modernity.* Waco: Baylor University Press, 2007.